11+ Verbal Reasoning
Study and Practice Book

Siân Goodspeed

Name **Testimony**

Schofield&Sims

Contents

Contents

Introduction

Verbal reasoning is language-based problem-solving. It involves thinking about words, letters, patterns and **sequences**. Verbal reasoning skills are useful for school tests, such as the 11+. There are many types of verbal reasoning questions – covering, for example, spelling, word meanings, maths and code-breaking. The question types in this book are among the most common. Verbal reasoning skills are important in other aspects of life too. Practising these skills expands your **vocabulary**, improves your spelling and develops your ability to use **logic**.

The topics are grouped into seven sections:

- word and letter patterns
- vocabulary
- grammar
- spelling
- cloze
- number patterns
- problem-solving.

You might not be tested on all these topics in your 11+ exam, but it is important to revise them in case they do come up.

If you are sitting an 11+ exam set by CEM, the verbal reasoning sections of your exam may include some comprehension questions. You will be asked to read a passage and answer some questions about it. Explanations and examples of comprehension questions can be found in the **11+ English Study and Practice Book**, which is also available from Schofield & Sims.

How to use this book

Before you start using this book, write your name in the box on the first page. Then decide how to begin. If you want a complete course in verbal reasoning, work right through the book. If you want to find out about a particular type of question, use the Contents page or the Index to find the pages you need. Whichever way you choose to use the book, don't try to cover too much at once – it is better to work in short bursts.

When you are ready to begin, find some rough paper. You may find this useful for your workings out. As you make a start, look out for the symbols below, which mark different parts of the text. Find out about words in **grey** by turning to the Glossary on pages 159 to 160.

Activities

These are the questions that you should complete after you have read the explanations and examples for each question type. After you have worked through all the questions, turn to pages 142 to 158 to check your answers. If you got any of the answers wrong, read the topic again, and then have another go at the questions. When you are sure that you understand a topic, tick the box beside it on the Contents page.

Tip

This text gives you helpful tips on how to tackle a particular question type.

Important

This text gives you useful information, rules and techniques you should remember.

At the end of the book, there is a 1-hour Practice test. You should attempt this once you are sure that you understand all the question types.

Schofield & Sims

Alphabet positions

These questions test your knowledge of the alphabet. You may be asked about the position of a letter in the alphabet or you might have to **identify** a letter from clues you are given about its position in a word.

You may be given the alphabet to help you. If you are not, you should write the alphabet out on your question paper.

If you are asked about the position of a letter in the alphabet, you will have to count up or down the alphabet in order to find it.

If the alphabet was written backwards, which letter would be at position 9?

Count backwards from **Z**. **Z** is at position 1, **Y** is at position 2, and so on. The answer is **R** because, counting backwards, **R** is at position 9.

Answer: R

 Now answer the following questions.

1. Which letter is at position 14 in the alphabet? ____

2. Which letter is at position 21 in the alphabet? ____

3. If the alphabet was written backwards, which letter would be at position 15? ____

 TIP Remember that the alphabet has 26 letters. Think about whether it will be quicker to count up or down through the alphabet to the position you are asked for. It may save time if you write numbers above the alphabet from 1 to 26 and below from 26 to 1.

Some questions might ask you to identify a letter using its position in a word and then to find the position of this letter in the alphabet.

Find the alphabet position of the letter that is in the middle of the word **CHEMISTRY**.

First, find the middle letter of **CHEMISTRY**. Cross out the first and last letters of the word, then the second and second last letters, and so on, until you are left with one letter in the middle.

C̶H̶E̶M̶I̶S̶T̶R̶Y̶   The middle letter of **CHEMISTRY** is **I**.

Now count through the alphabet until you find the position of the letter **I**. The answer is 9.

Answer: 9

 Now answer the following questions.

4. Find the alphabet position of the letter that is in the middle of the word **BUZZARD**. ____

5. Find the alphabet position of the letter that is in the middle of the word **WONDERFUL**. ____

6. Find the alphabet position of the letter that is in the middle of the word **TROUBLING**. ____

Alphabet positions

Sometimes, you might be asked to remove certain letters from the alphabet and then work out the position of one of the remaining letters. To answer this type of question, lightly cross out the letters you have been told to remove from the alphabet and then count through the remaining letters until you find the position of the letter you have been asked to find.

If the letters that spell **GORGEOUS** were removed from the alphabet, which letter would be in position 8 of the new alphabet?

A B C D E̶ F G̶ H I J K L M N O̶ P Q R̶ S̶ T U̶ V W X Y Z
1 2 3 4   5   6 7 8

The answer is **J** because it is at position 8 of the new alphabet.

Answer: J

 Now answer the following questions.

7.   If the letters that spell **SPOOKED** were removed from the alphabet, which letter would be in position 15 of the new alphabet?   ____

8.   If the letters that spell **RULING** were removed from the alphabet, which letter would be in position 12 of the new alphabet?   ____

9.   If the letters that spell **POISONS** were removed from the alphabet, which letter would be in position 17 of the new alphabet?   ____

Some questions might ask you to identify a letter in a word using a clue.

Which letter appears most often in the word **INSPIRATION**?

Count how many of each letter there are in the word and find the letter that appears most often. To help you keep count, use a tally chart and lightly cross off each letter in the word once you have counted it.

I	N	S	P	R	A	T	O
///	//	/	/	/	/	/	/

The answer is **I** because it appears more often than any other letter.

Answer: I

 Now answer the following questions.

10. Which letter appears most often in the word **NONSENSE**? ____

11. Which letter appears most often in the word **SYLLABLES**? ____

12. Which letter appears most often in the word **ECCENTRIC**? ____

Alphabet positions

Sometimes, you might have to use clues about a number of different words to identify a letter.

Find the letter that appears twice in **THREATEN**, once in **ENTHUSIASM** and once in **FLUTTER**.

Look at the first word, **THREATEN**.

Count how many times each letter appears in the word and find the letter or letters that appear twice.

Remember that you can use a tally chart to help you.

T	H	R	E	A	N
//	/	/	//	/	/

The letters **T** and **E** both appear twice. Either of those letters could be the answer.

Now look at the second word, **ENTHUSIASM**.

Cross out the letters that are not **T** or **E**, as these cannot be the answer.

E̶N̶T̶H̶U̶S̶I̶A̶S̶M̶

You can now see that **T** and **E** both appear once. Either of these letters could still be the answer.

Now look at the third word, **FLUTTER**.

Cross out the letters that are not **T** or **E**.

F̶L̶U̶T̶T̶E̶R̶

You can now see that **T** appears twice but **E** only appears once, so **E** must be the answer.

Answer: E

 Now answer the following questions.

13. Find the letter that appears twice in **DEVASTATES**, three times in **ESSENCES** and once in **DETERMINES**. ____

14. Find the letter that appears twice in **HORSESHOE**, once in **HOBBLES** and twice in **HUMOROUS**. ____

15. Find the letter that appears twice in **MOREOVER**, once in **MONOCHROME** and twice in **METEOROID**. ____

Sometimes, a clue might be about all the letters in a word.

> Which of the words below contains only the first **six** letters of the alphabet?
>
> acre   decide   faded   chase   fable
>
> List the first six letters of the alphabet – a, b, c, d, e, f – and compare each of the words to your list. For each word, lightly cross out any letters that appear on your list.
>
> ~~a~~ ~~c~~ r ~~e~~   Since not all of the letters of the word **acre** have been crossed out, it cannot be the answer. Repeat the process with each of the words until you find the word that has all of its letters crossed out.
>
> ~~f~~ ~~a~~ ~~d~~ ~~e~~ ~~d~~   It does not matter that some of the first six letters of the alphabet have not been used. What matters is that all the letters in the word are from the first six letters.
>
> **Answer: faded**

 Find the word in each group that contains only the first **six** letters of the alphabet.

16. died   beam   caged   bead   dial   _____

17. embed   decade   eras   eased   paid   _____

18. based   edged   ebbed   cawed   baked   _____

Sometimes, you might have to answer a question that involves both clues about the letters in a word and finding the position of letters in the alphabet.

> Which letter in the day of the week that begins with the letter nearest to the beginning of the alphabet is closest to the letter **S**?
>
> The days of the week begin with the letters **M**, **T**, **W**, **T**, **F** and **S**. Out of these, **F** is closest to the beginning of the alphabet so the word must be **FRIDAY**.
>
> Next, look at the letters of **FRIDAY** and identify which letter is closest to **S** in the alphabet. **R** is closest to **S** in the alphabet so **R** is the answer.
>
> **Answer: R**

 Now answer the following questions.

19. Which letter of the alphabet is **three** places after the position of the letter that appears most frequently in the word **TRIVIAL**? ____

20. Which letter of the alphabet is **two** places before the position of the letter that appears most frequently in the word **PRESSURES**? ____

21. Which of the months that begin with the letter that is closest to the beginning of the alphabet ends with the letter that is closest to the end of the alphabet? _____

Alphabetical order

These questions test your ability to **order** letters and words alphabetically.

If the letters in the word **DELIBERATES** are arranged in alphabetical order, which letter comes in the middle?

Work through the alphabet letter by letter, saying each letter in your head and comparing it to the word **DELIBERATES**. When you reach a letter that is present in **DELIBERATES**, write it down on rough paper. Make sure to write it down the same number of times as it appears in the word. Lightly cross out each letter in the word as you write it down.

Working through the alphabet, **a** appears in the word once, **b** appears once, **d** appears once, **e** appears three times, **i** appears once, **l** appears once, **r** appears once, **s** appears once and **t** appears once.

Your working should look like this:

~~deliberates~~

a b d e e e i l r s t

Now that the letters are in order, you must find the letter in the middle. Lightly cross out the first and last letters in your list, then the second and second last, third and third last and so on. You will be left with one letter in the middle.

~~a b d e e~~ e ~~i l r s t~~

The letter in the middle is **e**, so this is the answer.

Answer: e

 All the letters in the word should be crossed out. If you have missed any, go back over your list and put them in the correct place. Check that you have the same number of letters in your alphabetically ordered list of letters as there are in the word you started with.

 Now answer the following questions.

1. If the letters in the word **PRIVILEGE** are arranged in alphabetical order, which letter comes in the middle? ____

2. If the letters in the word **CORNERING** are arranged in alphabetical order, which letter comes in the middle? ____

3. If the letters in the word **SPECIALLY** are arranged in alphabetical order, which letter comes in the middle? ____

4. If the letters in the word **EMERGENCY** are arranged in alphabetical order, which letter comes in the middle? ____

5. If the letters in the word **COMPLICATED** are arranged in alphabetical order, which letter comes in the middle? ____

6. If the letters in the word **IMMERSIVE** are arranged in alphabetical order, which letter comes in the middle? ____

Alphabetical order

Some questions may ask you to put lists of words into alphabetical order and then find the position of a particular word in the alphabetically ordered list.

If these words were placed in alphabetical order, which word would be third in the list?

tailor   thought   taller   through   talking

Write the words in a column, taking care to line up each of the letters.

t a i l o r

t h o u g h t

t a l l e r

t h r o u g h

t a l k i n g

Now work through the columns of letters, from left to right, comparing the letters.

In the first column, all the words start with **t**, so this does not help us to put the words into alphabetical order.

In the second column, three of the words have **a** as their second letter and two have **h**. The three words with **a** as their second letter will come before the other two when they are placed in order.

In the third column, compare the third letters in each of the words that have **a** as their second letter. The third letter of **tailor** is **i**, the third letter of **taller** is **l** and the third letter of **talking** is **l**. **i** comes before **l** in the alphabet, so **tailor** will be first in the alphabetically ordered list.

Write the number 1 in a circle next to **tailor**. Then move on to compare the fourth letters of **taller** and **talking**. **k** comes before **l**, so **talking** will be the second word in the list and **taller** will be the third. Write the number 2 in a circle next to **talking** and the number 3 in a circle next to **taller**.

Now compare the third letters of the two words that have **h** as their second letter. **o** comes before **r**, so **thought** will be fourth in the list and **through** will be fifth. Write the numbers 4 and 5 in a circle next to these words.

t a i l o r   ①

t h o u g h t   ④

t a l l e r   ③

t h r o u g h   ⑤

t a l k i n g   ②

TIP You will have seen as you read through this example that you could have identified **taller** as the answer without putting the remaining words into alphabetical order. As long as you work carefully and you are sure that you have not made a mistake, there is no need to order all of the words if you have already found the answer.

taller is number 3, so you know it is third in the list when the words are alphabetically ordered. **taller** is the answer.

Answer: taller

! You might be asked to put the words in **reverse** alphabetical order, starting with the word that is closest to the end of the alphabet and working backwards. Use the same method to list the words in alphabetical order and then reverse the list so that the last word in the list becomes the first word, the second-last word becomes the second, and so on.

Schofield & Sims

Alphabetical order

Other questions might ask you to spell the words backwards and then order the words alphabetically. Use the same method as before, but write the words backwards underneath one another. You should still compare the columns working from left to right, from the first column to the last column.

If these words were spelt backwards and then placed in alphabetical order, which word would be last in the list?

tailor   thought   taller   through   talking

r o l i a t   ④
t h g u o h t   ⑤
r e l l a t   ③
h g u o r h t   ②
g n i k l a t   ①

The last word in the list when the answers are spelt backwards and ordered alphabetically is **thought**, so this is the answer.

Answer: thought

Now answer the following questions.

7. If these words were placed in alphabetical order, which word would be fourth in the list?

    hated   having   hatch   hassle   havoc   _____

8. If these words were placed in alphabetical order, which word would be fifth in the list?

    create   credit   crawl   crater   creeps   crack   _____

9. If these words were placed in reverse alphabetical order, which word would be second in the list?

    evoke   awake   slake   shale   shake   spoke   _____

10. If these words were placed in reverse alphabetical order, which word would be fifth in the list?

    motifs   motive   mourns   motors   mouths   motion   _____

11. If these words were spelt backwards and then placed in alphabetical order, which word would be third in the list?

    girder   murder   wonder   border   louder   spider   _____

12. If these words were spelt backwards and then placed in alphabetical order, which word would be last in the list?

    canary   binary   salary   granary   library   unwary   _____

Here you are given a **series** of letters. You need to look for a pattern and find the next two letters. An alphabet is given to help you.

A B C D E F G H I J K L M N O P Q R S T U V W X Y Z

Find the next two letters in the series.

SW UY WA YC AE (____ ____)

Look at the first letters of each pair. Count the jumps between them. For example, there are two jumps in the alphabet between **S** and **U**.

Write the numbers above the sequence. This makes it easier to spot a pattern. Use **+** for forwards jumps. Use **−** for backwards jumps.

Do the same for the second letters of each pair. Count the jumps. Write the numbers.

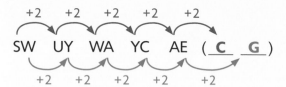

When you have found the pattern, you can write the final pair of numbers.

Answer: CG

Look out for different types of pattern when solving letter sequences.

Forwards and backwards movements

Find the next two letters in the series.

PT MV JX GZ DB (____ ____)

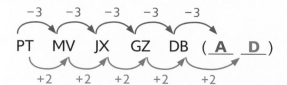

Here, the jumps go backwards from one letter and forwards from the other.

Answer: AD

 Find the next two letters in each series. The alphabet above will help you.

1. JP KR LT MV NX (____ ____)

2. QE NH KK HN EQ (____ ____)

3. ZA YB XC WD VE (____ ____)

4. FF HE JD LC NB (____ ____)

 TIP If you are **jumping forwards** and you reach **Z** with more letters to go, carry on from **A** again. Count **Z** to **A** as one step. If you are **jumping backwards** from **A**, go to **Z**. This also counts as one step. It may help if you add three or four letters to either end of the alphabet, like this:

W X Y Z A B C D E F G H I J K L M N O P Q R S T U V W X Y Z A B C D

Here are three other pattern types to look out for.

Increasing or decreasing gaps

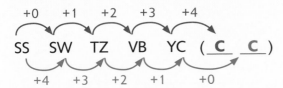

Here, the number of letters in a jump increases between the first letters of each pair. It decreases between the second letters.

Answer: CC

Alternating gaps

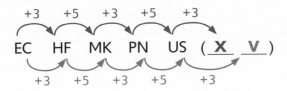

Sometimes, the gaps **alternate**. Here, they go in turns between three jumps and five jumps.

Answer: XV

 Find the next two letters in each series. Use the alphabet on page 12 to help you.

5.   MO PR QS TV UW (___ ___)

6.   TU YZ CD FG HI (___ ___)

7.   QP OO NM LL KJ (___ ___)

8.   HJ GK EM BP XT (___ ___)

Leapfrogging

If there are more than eight jumps between letters or if they seem to follow no obvious pattern, look for **two** patterns that **leapfrog** over each other.

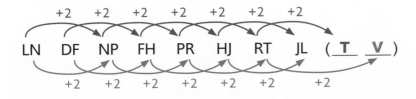

With leapfrogging sequences, always make sure you jump over the last pair of letters to get to the answer.

Answer: TV

 Find the next two letters in each series. Use the alphabet on page 12 to help you.

9.   AC SU DF VX GI YA (___ ___)

10. PO DC ML BA JI ZY (___ ___)

11. RO FD SP GE UR IG XU LJ (___ ___)

12. PT DC OS FE LP GF KO IH (___ ___)

 TIP Learn to continue the alphabet from any point. Knowing it backwards will help too.

Letters missing from the beginning of a sequence

In some questions, the missing letters may be at the beginning of the sequence. In these cases, use the same strategies as before to work out the **connection** between the letter pairs you have been given and find the missing letters.

Find the missing pair of letters.

(___ ___) YD   AF   CH   EJ

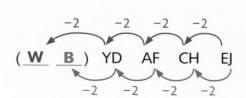

Count the jumps from the first letters in each pair and then the second letters. There are two jumps in between each letter. In order to find the first pair, you therefore need to count back two from each letter: **Y** jumps back two letters to **W**; **D** jumps back two letters to **B**, so the answer is **WB**. You can then double-check your answer is correct by counting forwards two jumps from **W** and two jumps from **B** to make sure the next pair in the sequence is **YD**.

Answer: WB

 Find the missing pair of letters in each series. Use the alphabet below to help you.

A B C D E F G H I J K L M N O P Q R S T U V W X Y Z

13. (___ ___) FT IU LV OW

14. (___ ___) RP QO PN OM

15. (___ ___) ZX DB GE IG

16. (___ ___) DG BL ZQ XV

Letters missing from the middle of a sequence

In some questions, the missing letters may be elsewhere in the sequence. Again, use the same strategies to work out the pattern between the **consecutive** letters and apply the same rule to the pair of letters before and after the gap to work out the missing pair.

Find the missing pair of letters.

IL JM LO (___ ___) SV XA

The gap between the letters is +1 then +2. This could either be a repeating pattern or an increasing gap so you need to check the gap between the next two pairs of letters you have been given. We can see this is +5 so we can conclude that this is a sequence with an increasing gap, meaning that the missing pair of letters can be found by jumping forwards three letters from **L** and **O**. The answer is therefore **OR**.

Answer: OR

 Find the missing pair of letters in each series.

17. HR JT KU (___ ___) NX PZ

18. LA QF (___ ___) XM ZO

19. OE NF (___ ___) IK EO

20. PN QO (___ ___) VT ZX

Letter codes

In these questions, you work out how two pairs of letters are connected. Then you find the pair of letters that go with a third pair of letters in the same way.

> Find the letters that complete the sentence in the best way.
>
> **BE** is to **YV** as **GJ** is to ____ ____

There are two ways of solving letter codes questions: one way for questions involving letter partners, and one way for questions involving jumping.

Letter partners questions are described below. Jumping questions are described on page 17.

Letter partners

Every letter in the first half of the alphabet has a partner in the second half. You draw a line down the centre of the alphabet, between **M** and **N**. Then you number it as shown below.

A	B	C	D	E	F	G	H	I	J	K	L	M	N	O	P	Q	R	S	T	U	V	W	X	Y	Z
1	2	3	4	5	6	7	8	9	10	11	12	13	13	12	11	10	9	8	7	6	5	4	3	2	1

Any two letters with the same number under them are letter partners. For example, **A** and **Z** are both numbered 1, so they are letter partners. **L** and **O** are both numbered 12, so they are letter partners.

This is sometimes called the **mirror technique**. Each letter's partner is 'reflected' in the central line.

Find the letter partner of each of the following. Use the alphabet above to help you.

1. B ____

2. L ____

3. G ____

4. U ____

5. O ____

6. S ____

7. I ____

8. X ____

9. E ____

10. W ____

11. N ____

12. K ____

TIP It is a good idea to learn the partner of each letter of the alphabet by heart (**A** goes with **Z**, **B** goes with **Y**, **C** goes with **X**, and so on). This will help you to spot letter partner questions more quickly.

Letter codes

You can now work through the Letter partners question introduced at the top of page 15.

Find the letters that complete the sentence in the best way.

BE is to **YV** as **GJ** is to ____ ____

Look at the first pair of letters. Check whether their partners are in the second pair.

A (B) C D (E) F G H I J K L M | N O P Q R S T U (V) W X (Y) Z
1 (2) 3 4 (5) 6 7 8 9 10 11 12 13 | 13 12 11 10 9 8 7 6 (5) 4 3 (2) 1

B has 2 under it. So does **Y**. So **B** and **Y** are letter partners.

E and **V** both have 5 under them, so they are letter partners too. We now know that this is a Letter partners question.

Find the partners of each of the letters in the third pair, **GJ**, by looking at the other half of the alphabet.

G = 7. The other letter with a 7 under it is **T**.

J = 10. The other letter with a 10 under it is **Q**.

Answer: TQ

Sometimes, the first and second letters of each pair are reversed.

For example: **BE** (2, 5) is to **VY** (5, 2) as **GJ** (7, 10) is to ____ ____   **Answer: QT** (10, 7)

Find the letters that complete the sentence in the best way. Use the alphabet below to help you.

A B C D E F G H I J K L M | N O P Q R S T U V W X Y Z
1 2 3 4 5 6 7 8 9 10 11 12 13 | 13 12 11 10 9 8 7 6 5 4 3 2 1

13. **LF** is to **OU** as **RS** is to ____ ____

14. **PR** is to **KI** as **VX** is to ____ ____

15. **CB** is to **YX** as **LP** is to ____ ____

16. **HE** is to **VS** as **UZ** is to ____ ____

17. **MO** is to **NL** as **RD** is to ____ ____

18. **AJ** is to **QZ** as **KL** is to ____ ____

19. **IU** is to **RF** as **LT** is to ____ ____

20. **JD** is to **QW** as **YG** is to ____ ____

Schofield & Sims

Letter codes

Jumping

Some letter codes questions involve jumping.

Find the letters that complete the sentence in the best way.

CX is to **DW** as **HS** is to ___ ___

First, check to see if this is a Letter partners question (see pages 15 and 16).

C and **D** are not letter partners. Neither are **X** and **W**. This must therefore be a Jumping question.

Write the **first** pair of letters above the **second** pair:

CX

DW

Count the jumps from the top letter to the one below. Use **+** for forwards and **−** for backwards jumps. First count **C** to **D**, then **X** to **W**.

Look at the purple arrows. The first letter jumps forwards by 1. The second letter jumps backwards by 1.

```
     +1                                              −1
    ⌒→                                              ⌒→
A  B  C  D  E  F  G  H  I  J  K  L  M  N  O  P  Q  R  S  T  U  V  W  X  Y  Z
              ↳↗                              ↳↗
             +1                              −1
```

Now apply the same number of jumps (+1 then −1) to the third pair, **HS**.

Look at the green arrows. **H** + 1 is **I** and **S** − 1 is **R**.   **Answer: IR**

Find the letters that complete the sentence in the best way. Use the alphabet below to help you.

A	B	C	D	E	F	G	H	I	J	K	L	M	N	O	P	Q	R	S	T	U	V	W	X	Y	Z
1	2	3	4	5	6	7	8	9	10	11	12	13	13	12	11	10	9	8	7	6	5	4	3	2	1

21. **CE** is to **FH** as **DF** is to ___ ___

22. **LO** is to **JM** as **PS** is to ___ ___

23. **DD** is to **GB** as **JJ** is to ___ ___

24. **MS** is to **RW** as **DH** is to ___ ___

25. **SU** is to **KM** as **WZ** is to ___ ___

26. **EC** is to **JX** as **OM** is to ___ ___

27. **CT** is to **KR** as **NJ** is to ___ ___

28. **LW** is to **IA** as **PZ** is to ___ ___

Word codes questions are similar to letter codes questions. You are given a word and have to find the code, or you are given a code and have to work out the word.

As with letter codes questions, there are two techniques for solving word codes questions: letter partners and jumping. Letter partners questions are described below and on page 19. Jumping questions are described on pages 20 and 21.

Letter partners – find the code

> If the code for **CRAB** is **XIZY**, what is the code for **FISH**?
>
> | A | B | C | D | E | F | G | H | I | J | K | L | M | N | O | P | Q | R | S | T | U | V | W | X | Y | Z |
> |---|---|---|---|---|---|---|---|---|---|---|---|---|---|---|---|---|---|---|---|---|---|---|---|---|---|
> | 1 | 2 | 3 | 4 | 5 | 6 | 7 | 8 | 9 | 10 | 11 | 12 | 13 | 13 | 12 | 11 | 10 | 9 | 8 | 7 | 6 | 5 | 4 | 3 | 2 | 1 |
>
> Number the alphabet. Is this a Letter partners question? The first letter in **CRAB** is partners with the first letter in the code **XIZY**. **C** = 3 and **X** = 3, so they are letter partners.
>
> Check the other letters in **CRAB** and **XIZY** are partners. **R** = 9 and **I** = 9, **A** = 1 and **Z** = 1, **B** = 2 and **Y** = 2. They are all letter partners. This is a Letter partners question.
>
> Now use the alphabet to work out the code for **FISH**.
>
> **F** = 6.   The other letter numbered 6 is **U**. So, **U** is the code letter for **F**.
>
> **I** = 9.   The other letter numbered 9 is **R**. So, **R** is the code letter for **I**.
>
> **S** = 8.   The other letter numbered 8 is **H**. So, **H** is the code letter for **S**.
>
> **H** = 8.   The other letter numbered 8 is **S**. So, **S** is the code letter for **H**.
>
> **Answer: URHS**

 Now answer the following questions. Use the alphabet above to help you.

1. If the code for **SHEEP** is **HSVVK**, what is the code for **COWS**? _____

2. If the code for **DANCE** is **WZMXV**, what is the code for **SING**? _____

3. If **TRAIN** is written in code as **GIZRM**, what is the code for **COACH**? _____

4. If **HORSE** in code is **SLIHV**, what is the code for **PONY**? _____

5. If the code for **HAPPY** is **SZKKB**, what is the code for **ANGRY**? _____

6. If **ANIMAL** is written in code as **ZMRNZO**, what is the code for **INSECT**? _____

Letter partners – find the word

> If the code for **STAR** is **HGZI**, what does **NLLM** mean?

Number the alphabet. Is this a Letter partners question (see page 15)?

A	B	C	D	E	F	G	H	I	J	K	L	M	N	O	P	Q	R	S	T	U	V	W	X	Y	Z
1	2	3	4	5	6	7	8	9	10	11	12	13	13	12	11	10	9	8	7	6	5	4	3	2	1

The **S** in **STAR** is partners with the **H** in **HGZI**. The other letters are partners too. So, this is a Letter partners question.

Now find the partner for each letter in the code **NLLM**.

N = 13 and **M** = 13, so the first letter of the word is **M**.

L is partners with **O** and **M** is partners with **N**.

Answer: MOON

TIP You can number the alphabet to see which letters are letter partners. Or, instead of numbering, you can write the first half of the alphabet backwards under the second half, like the example below. This can also help you see which letters are partners.

Now answer the following questions. Use the alphabet below to help you.

A	B	C	D	E	F	G	H	I	J	K	L	M	N	O	P	Q	R	S	T	U	V	W	X	Y	Z
													M	L	K	J	I	H	G	F	E	D	C	B	A

7. If the code for **FARM** is **UZIN**, what does **BZIW** mean? _____

8. If **NIGHT** is written in code as **MRTSG**, what does **WZIP** mean? _____

9. If **HOVVK** is the code for **SLEEP**, what does **WIVZN** mean? _____

10. If **NLMPVB** in code means **MONKEY**, what does **TRIZUUV** mean? _____

11. If **PILOT** is written in code as **KROLG**, what does **KOZMV** mean? _____

12. If the code for **UNDER** is **FMWVI**, what does **ZYLFG** mean? _____

Jumping – find the code

If the question is not a Letter partners question, use the Jumping technique, as with Letter codes questions.

If the code for **SAND** is **UCPF**, what is the code for **SEA**?

Check to see if it is a Letter partners question (see page 15). It is not.

It is a Jumping question (see page 17). You are looking for a code. Write the first code. Then write the first word above the code:

SAND

UCPF

Count the jumps from the top letter to the one below. Use **+** for forwards and **−** for backwards jumps. Count **S** to **U**, then work through the other letters: **A** to **C**, **N** to **P** and **D** to **F**.

Look at the purple arrows and numbers. Each letter jumps forwards by 2.

Now apply the same numbers of jumps (+2) to the third item in the question, **SEA**.
Look at the green arrows.

S + 2 = U

E + 2 = G

A + 2 = C

Answer: UGC

 Now answer the following questions. Use the alphabet below to help you.

A B C D E F G H I J K L M N O P Q R S T U V W X Y Z

13. If the code for **BLUE** is **CMVF**, what is the code for **GREEN**? _____

14. If **KNTC** is the code for **LOUD**, what is the code for **QUIET**? _____

15. If the code for **GRASS** is **HTDWX**, what is the code for **TREE**? _____

16. If **PARTY** is written in code as **OWQPX**, what is the code for **FEAST**? _____

17. If the code for **HISTORY** is **KHVSRQB**, what is the code for **SCIENCE**?_____

18. If **LORRY** is written in code as **QJWMD**, what is the code for **TRUCK**? _____

Jumping – find the word

If the code for **SHOE** is **TJRI**, what does **TQFO** mean?

TIP To find a **code**, write the **first code**, then write the **first word** above it. To find a **word**, write the **first word**, then write the **first code** above it.

Is this a Letter partners question (see page 15)? It is not.
It is a Jumping question (see page 17). You are looking for a word.
Write the first word. Then write the first code above the word:

T J R I
S H O E

Count the jumps from the top letter to the one below. Use **+** for forwards and **–** for backwards jumps. Count **T** to **S**, then work through the other letters: **J** to **H**, **R** to **O** and **I** to **E**.

Look at the purple arrows. Each letter jumps backwards – by 1, then 2, then 3, then 4.

A B C D E F G H I J K L M N O P Q R S T U V W X Y Z

Apply the same jumps to the third item, **TQFO**. Look at the green arrows.   **Answer: SOCK**

 Now answer the following questions. Use the alphabet on page 20 to help you.

19. If **TREE** in code is **USFF**, what does **CVTI** mean?   _____

20. If **JCPM** means **LARK** in code, what does **EWJN** mean?   _____

21. If **WHISPER** in code is **YGKRRDT**, what does **NZWFJSGQ** mean?   _____

Use the same strategies if symbols are used instead of letters.

If **!*&^£** is the code for **PRICE**, what is the code for **RIP**?

To work out the answer, simply write the code symbols above each letter in the word:

! * & ^ £
P R I C E

Then work out which symbols represent each of the letters in the word **RIP**.   **Answer: *&!**

 Now answer the following questions.

22. If **DAIRY** is written in code as **$! " ^ ?**, what is the code for **RAID**?   _____

23. If **PREVENT** in code is ☺✋☼✎☼⌂🕯, what does 🕯☼⌂🕯 mean?   _____

24. If the code for **SPEAK** is *** $! ? +**, what does **? $!** mean?   _____

In these questions, you are given four words and three number codes. Each code goes with one of the words. The same numbers represent the same letters in all of them. One code is missing.

R A I L   M E A L   R A I N   M A I L

     7 3 5 1   2 3 5 8   7 9 3 1

First, you need to work out which code goes with which word.

Look for letters that the words have **in common**. Look for numbers that the codes have in common. Start with the letters at the end or the beginning of the words.

Once you have matched a number to a letter, write the number above that letter every time it appears.

Three of the words end in **L** and two of the codes end in 1. So, **L** is represented by 1. You can write it in.

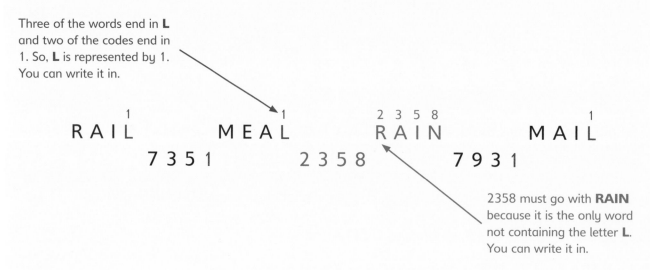

    1   1   2 3 5 8   1
R A I L   M E A L   R A I N   M A I L

    7 3 5 1   2 3 5 8   7 9 3 1

2358 must go with **RAIN** because it is the only word not containing the letter **L**. You can write it in.

Next, you need to match the codes you are given to their words.

Now you can write in the code numbers wherever else you see **R**, **A**, **I** or **N**.

2 3 5 1   7 9 3 1   2 3 5 8   7 3 5 1
R A I L   M E A L   R A I N   M A I L

    7 3 5 1   2 3 5 8   7 9 3 1

You know that the full code that ends 31 is 7931. You know that the full code that ends 351 is 7351. Now you can write these in.

Finally, you can identify the word with the missing code.

The missing code is for **RAIL**. The code for **RAIL** is 2351.

Match the codes

Now that you have found all of the codes, you can answer the questions below.

2 3 5 1   7 9 3 1   2 3 5 8   7 3 5 1
R A I L   M E A L   R A I N   M A I L

7 3 5 1   2 3 5 8   7 9 3 1

i)   What is the code for **MANE**?

Look at the numbers above each of these letters.

M is 7, **A** is 3, **N** is 8 and **E** is 9.   **Answer: 7389**

ii)   What does **7511** mean?

Look at the letter below each of these numbers.

7 is **M**, 5 is **I** and 1 is **L**.   **Answer: MILL**

TIP   Look for letters that only appear in one word and numbers that only appear in one code.

Match the number codes to the words below. Then answer the questions.

1.   8 4 6 7   3 4 9 5   8 4 9 7
S H I P   C H O P   S H I N   C H I P

What are the codes for:

i)   **SHOP**? _____   ii)   **PINCH**? _____

2.   9 5 1 7   3 5 1 9   9 8 4 1
S I N G   G A I N   G O N E   S O N G

What are the codes for:

i)   **SOON**? _____   ii)   **AGAIN**? _____

3.   4 3 6 2   4 5 2 1   1 7 3 2
T R A P   P O R T   P A I R   T E A R

i)   What does **4321** mean? _____

ii)   What is the code for **TERROR**? _____

Make a word from one other word

In these questions, you are given two pairs of words and a question word. In each pair, the second word is made using some of the letters in the first word. The position of the letters is the same for both pairs.

You work out the position of the second word within the first word. Then you find the letters that are in the same position in the question word. You make a word from them.

Working from left to right

In these questions the second words are easy to spot.

Look at the first pair of words. Find the pattern.

Here are three pairs of words. The third pair of words is made in the same way as the first two pairs. Find the missing word and write it on the line.

(mask ask)   (band and)   (stop _____)

ask is made from **mask** by dropping the first letter.

and is made by dropping the first letter of **band**.

Therefore, to find the answer, drop the **s** in **stop**.

Answer: top

(!) Letters may be added to or removed from any position, not just the beginning or end of the word.

 In these questions there are three pairs of words. The third pair of words is made in the same way as the first two pairs. Find the missing word and write it on the line.

1. (pant pan)   (band ban)   (seem _____)

2. (tram ram)   (twin win)   (boat _____)

3. (hop shop)   (aid said)   (ash _____)

4. (many man)   (seed see)   (lady _____)

5. (all ball)   (ore pore)   (ear _____)

6. (grown gown)   (steal seal)   (black _____)

7. (table tale)   (tire tie)   (bleed _____)

8. (grain rain)   (tread read)   (cloud _____)

9. (bend bed)   (sand sad)   (burn _____)

10. (tramp trap)   (grind grid)   (beard _____)

Schofield & Sims

Make a word from one other word

Taking letters from any position

These questions involve taking letters from any position in the first word to make the second word. The letters may not necessarily be used in the same order as in the first word.

Here are three pairs of words. The third pair of words is made in the same way as the first two pairs. Find the missing word and write it on the line.

(brings gin)   (shield lie)   (glares _____)

First, number the letters in the word **brings**.

Use the second pair to check your answer.

1 2 3 4 5 6   5 3 4
(b r i n g s /g i n)

1 2 3 4 5 6   5 3 4
(s h i e l d   l i e)

1 2 3 4 5 6   5 3 4
(g l a r e s   e a r)

Then number the letters in the word **gin** according to their position in the word **brings**.

Number the letters in **glares**.

Take the letters from the same position as in the earlier pairs (534). 5 = **e**, 3 = **a**, 4 = **r**.

Answer: ear

TIP   Remember that the second set of words always follows the same pattern as the first set.

In these questions there are three pairs of words. The third pair of words is made in the same way as the first two pairs. Find the missing word and write it on the line.

11. (party trap)   (stare rats)   (liver _____)

12. (tinsel lint)   (leaded deal)   (denies _____)

13. (amused muse)   (staked take)   (phoned _____)

14. (crawls law)   (growls low)   (tootle _____)

15. (please slap)   (treads drat)   (brought _____)

16. (around ran)   (apart pat)   (abound _____)

17. (trail rat)   (though hot)   (troop _____)

18. (ground rod)   (spoilt pot)   (stolen _____)

19. (ambush ham)   (inward din)   (aghast _____)

20. (adrift rift)   (entail tail)   (appear _____)

Make a word from one other word

Words with repeated letters

Sometimes, one or more of the letters in the second word are found in more than one place in the first word.

Here are three pairs of words. The third pair of words is made in the same way as the first two pairs. Find the missing word and write it on the line.

(classes sale)   (hounds duos)   (blurred _____)

First, number the letters in **classes**.

Then number the letters in the word **sale** according to their position in **classes**. **s** appears three times. Write all three numbers above **s**.

4
5

1 2 3 4 5 6 7   7 3 2 6
(c l a s s e s   s a l e)

Number the second pair in the same way. Notice that the first letter of the second word is taken from position 5 (not 4 or 7) because that is the position of the letter **d** in **hounds**.

1 2 3 4 5 6   5 3 2 6
(h o u n d s   d u o s)

1 2 3 4 5 6 7   5 3 2 6
(b l u r r e d   r u l e)

Number the letters in **blurred**.

Take the letters from positions 5326.
5 = **r**, 3 = **u**, 2 = **l**, 6 = **e**.

Answer: rule

In these questions there are three pairs of words. The third pair of words is made in the same way as the first two pairs. Find the missing word and write it on the line.

21. (bellow low)   (maggot got)   (barrow _____)

22. (juggle leg)   (muddle led)   (window _____)

23. (proper pope)   (weaker wake)   (fronds _____)

24. (stones nest)   (stewed west)   (deacon _____)

25. (dribble bile)   (bramble bale)   (whistle _____)

26. (asleep pale)   (haunts shun)   (instil _____)

27. (bottle lot)   (middle lid)   (toggle _____)

28. (doted dot)   (metal let)   (timed _____)

29. (dented dent)   (forest tore)   (lunged _____)

30. (denote teen)   (handle lean)   (galore _____)

Make a word from two other words

In these questions, you are given two groups of words. You must find the missing word from the second group.

Taking letters from any position

Here, the word in the middle of the first group is made using letters from the words on either side. Work out the position of the letters in the first group. Then make a word using the letters in the same positions in the second group.

> The word in the middle of the second group is made in the same way as the word in the middle of the first group. Find the word that is missing in the second group and write it on the line.
>
> (speak [spin] wine)   (train [_____] ripe)

Look at the middle word in the first group, **spin**. Identify where each letter of **spin** is found in **speak** and **wine**. Point at the letter in the middle word of the first group and then to its **location** in the words on either side. As you find each letter, go straight to the second group. Find the letter in the same position. Write the letters as you go.

The first letter of **spin** is found at the beginning of **speak**, so the missing word begins with the first letter of **train**, **t**.

The second letter of **spin** is found in the second position in **speak**. So, the second letter in the missing word is the second letter in the word **train**, **r**.

(speak [spin] wine)   (train [_tr___] ripe)

The third letter of **spin** is found in the second position in **wine**. So, the third letter in the missing word is the second letter in the word **ripe**, **i**.

(speak [spin] wine)   (train [_trip_] ripe)

Answer: trip

The last letter of **spin** is found in the third position in **wine**. So, the last letter in the missing word is the third letter in the word **ripe**, **p**.

 In these questions, the word in the middle of the second group is made in the same way as the word in the middle of the first group. Find the word that is missing in the second group and write it on the line.

1. (help [hear] pair)   (soup [_____] grit)

2. (night [this] sulk)   (cream [_____] entry)

3. (magic [aged] mode)   (lever [_____] line)

4. (shop [save] vane)   (pace [_____] alone)

5. (sound [done] lake)   (peels [_____] leaf)

6. (shower [wash] army)   (thumb [_____] open)

7. (hand [hint] site)   (lash [_____] moth)

8. (drop [dear] vase)   (clap [_____] halo)

Make a word from two other words

Words with repeated letters

Sometimes, one or more of the letters in the middle word can be found in more than one location in the outside words.

The word in the middle of the second group is made in the same way as the word in the middle of the first group. Find the word that is missing in the second group and write it on the line.

(temple [pine] into)   (frothy [_____] easy)

The first letter in **pine** comes from the fourth letter in **temple**, **p**. So, the first letter of the missing word comes from the fourth letter in **frothy**, **t**.

(temple [pine] into)   (frothy [_te_] easy)

The second letter in **pine** is the first letter of **into**, so the second letter of the missing word is **e**.

The third letter in **pine** is from the second letter in **into**, so the next missing letter is **a**.

(temple [pine] into)

____tear____

(temple [pine] into)   (frothy [_teay_] easy)

The last letter in **pine** is in the second **and** the sixth positions in the word **temple**. So, look at the second and sixth letters in the word **frothy**, **r** and **y**. Write one of the letters above the other to make the two words. Decide which is a real word.

TIP: If you are doing a multiple-choice paper and you come across alternative answers, check which option appears on the answer sheet.

Answer: tear (because **teay** is not a word)

In these questions, the word in the middle of the second group is made in the same way as the word in the middle of the first group. Find the word that is missing in the second group and write it on the line.

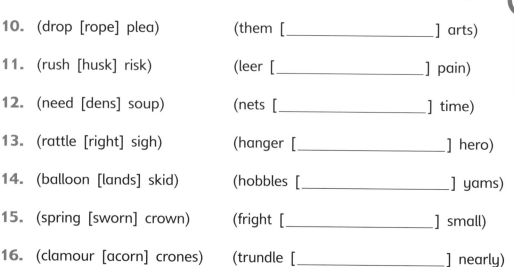

9.   (melt [test] spot)   (leap [_____] rink)

10. (drop [rope] plea)   (them [_____] arts)

11. (rush [husk] risk)   (leer [_____] pain)

12. (need [dens] soup)   (nets [_____] time)

13. (rattle [right] sigh)   (hanger [_____] hero)

14. (balloon [lands] skid)   (hobbles [_____] yams)

15. (spring [sworn] crown)   (fright [_____] small)

16. (clamour [acorn] crones) (trundle [_____] nearly)

⚠ There may be several repeated letters. You must write down **all** the letter options.

Schofield & Sims

Now test your skills with these practice pages. If you get stuck, go back to pages 5 to 28 for some reminders.

Alphabet positions

Use the alphabet to help you answer the questions below.

A B C D E F G H I J K L M N O P Q R S T U V W X Y Z

1. If the alphabet was written backwards, which letter would be at position 23? ____

2. Find the alphabet position of the letter that is in the middle of the word **ENVIRONMENT**. ____

3. If the letters that spell **DIGESTION** were removed from the alphabet, which letter would be in position 11 of the new alphabet? ____

4. Which letter appears most often in the word **ANTICIPATION**? ____

5. Find the letter that appears twice in **LENIENTLY**, twice in **LEISURELY** and twice in **FLEDGLINGS**. ____

Find the word in each group that contains only the first **six** letters of the alphabet.

6. feud   badge   beach   coded   deface   _____

7. erase   ceded   danced   diced   feeble   _____

8. Which day of the week begins with the letter that is halfway between the letters **i** and **q**? _____

Alphabetical order

Use the alphabet to help you answer the questions below.

A B C D E F G H I J K L M N O P Q R S T U V W X Y Z

9. If the letters in the word **JOCULARLY** are arranged in alphabetical order, which letter comes in the middle? ____

10. If the letters in the word **FRIGHTENING** are arranged in alphabetical order, which letter comes in the middle? ____

11. If the letters in the word **LEGENDARY** are arranged in alphabetical order, which letter comes in the middle? ____

12. If these words were placed in alphabetical order, which word would be third in the list?

    crown   cruel   crowd   crocus   crows   crock   _____

13. If these words were placed in reverse alphabetical order, which word would be fourth in the list?

    weight   wields   wider   weekly   weeping   whiter   _____

14. If these words were spelt backwards and then placed in alphabetical order, which word would be fifth in the list?

    disrupt   except   corrupt   receipt   exempt   excerpt   _____

Letter sequences

Find the missing pair of letters in each series. Use the alphabet below to help you.

A B C D E F G H I J K L M N O P Q R S T U V W X Y Z

1. LK NM PO RQ TS (___ ___)

2. VE UF TG SH RI (___ ___)

3. AE WX CG YZ EI AB GK (___ ___)

4. (___ ___) SU VR YO BL

5. (___ ___) JE NA RW VS

6. BV (___ ___) NJ GQ ZX

Letter codes

Find the letters that complete the sentence in the best way. Use the alphabet above to help you.

7. **AC** is to **DF** as **HJ** is to ___ ___

8. **SA** is to **ZH** as **MP** is to ___ ___

9. **CD** is to **XW** as **EF** is to ___ ___

10. **GJ** is to **IL** as **RU** is to ___ ___

11. **OQ** is to **RP** as **WV** is to ___ ___

12. **HB** is to **YS** as **PL** is to ___ ___

Word codes

Work out the code or word for each question below. Use the alphabet above to help you.

13. If the code for **APPLE** is **CQRMG**, what is the code for **ORANGE**? _____

14. If **DRAGON** in code is **CQZFNM**, how would **KNIGHT** be written? _____

15. If **KFWWOV** means **PUDDLE** in code, what does **WIRAAOV** mean? _____

16. If the code for **MELON** is **NGOSS**, what does **MGPSS** mean? _____

17. If **ALERT** is ☼ + & 🔔 💧 in code, what is the code for **LATTER**? _____

Match the codes

Match the number codes to the words below. Then answer the questions.

18.   1 4 8 7   3 4 6 3   3 4 5 1
   T H I S   T H A T   S H O W   W H A T

   i)   What is the code for **THIS**? _____

   ii) What is the code for **THAW**? _____

   iii) What does **7614** mean? _____

19.   9 1 3 6   6 8 9 1   6 8 7 3
   M O S T   S T E M   D O E S   M O D E

   i)   What is the code for **STEM**? _____

   ii) What is the code for **MOODS**? _____

   iii) What does **93379** mean? _____

Make a word from one other word

In these questions there are three pairs of words. The third pair of words is made in the same way as the first two pairs. Find the missing word and write it on the line.

1.   (west wet)   (best bet)   (fast _____)

2.   (chain chin)   (grain grin)   (breed _____)

3.   (waddle lad)   (little lit)   (meddle _____)

4.   (matron tram)   (poster stop)   (masher _____)

5.   (rampart ramp)   (lantern rant)   (mentors _____)

6.   (assures sure)   (redeems seem)   (staring _____)

7.   (shut hut)   (bran ran)   (grub _____)

8.   (bush bus)   (song son)   (team _____)

9.   (rotten not)   (mitten nit)   (logged _____)

10. (feast seat)   (clasp slap)   (hints _____)

Make a word from two other words

In these questions, the word in the middle of the second group is made in the same way as the word in the middle of the first group. Find the word that is missing in the second group and write it on the line.

11. (weed [tore] root)   (pies [_____] tall)

12. (white [with] trawl)   (height [_____] crane)

13. (wand [dawn] dear)   (bust [_____] tent)

14. (bangs [bond] bound)   (stale [_____] lines)

15. (flower [slow] houses)   (thanks [_____] hostels)

16. (windows [chins] coaches)   (barrage [_____] whisper)

17. (weep [pray] tray)   (door [_____] sing)

18. (table [grab] green)   (misty [_____] there)

19. (fancy [funny] haiku)   (burly [_____] prime)

20. (vines [invest] nest)   (ashen [_____] owls)

Word meanings

These questions test your vocabulary and your ability to use vocabulary, grammar and context clues to identify the meaning of words.

Read the sentence below and then answer the question that follows.

The two states were unified into a single country.

What does 'unified' mean?

A. divided

B. reigned

C. together

D. multimedia

E. merged

The wider your vocabulary, the more likely it is that you will be able to identify the meaning of the word. However, if the word is unfamiliar to you, there are strategies that you can use to work out the meaning.

A useful way to start is by reading the sentence and replacing the word you are asked to define with each of the multiple-choice options. Think about which of the sentences still make sense.

The two states were **divided** into a single country.

Two things can't be **divided** into one, so we can eliminate answer option **A**.

The two states were **reigned** into a single country.

It does make sense that a country could be reigned. However, the context of the sentence means that **reigned** does not make sense in this position, so we can eliminate answer option **B**.

The two states were **together** into a single country.

Two states could be brought together to become one. However, **together** does not fit the structure of the sentence. Since **unified** ends in **–ed**, it is probably a verb written in the past tense. **Together** is not a verb and so cannot replace **unified** in the sentence, so we can eliminate answer option **C**.

The two states were **multimedia** into a single country.

You may not know the definition of **multimedia**. A strategy you could use to help you here is to consider **prefixes**. Prefixes can give you useful clues about the meaning of words. The question asks for the meaning of **unified**. The prefix of **unified** is **uni–**, which means 'one'. The prefix of **multimedia** is **multi–**, which means 'many'. It is therefore very unlikely that the two words mean the same thing, so we can eliminate answer option **D**.

 TIP You can use the definitions of words that you already know to help you to identify the meaning of a prefix. For instance, to remind yourself what **uni–** means, remember that a unicorn has one horn, a unicycle has one wheel, and if something is unique there is only one of its kind. To remember what **multi–** means, remember that you will get more of something if you multiply it.

Schofield & Sims

The two states were **merged** into a single country.

By eliminating the other answer options, you are only left with answer option **E. Merged** makes sense in the sentence as it means 'joined together'. However, it is possible to work out that **merged** is the answer without knowing its exact definition. Always consider the type and tense of the word you are asked to define, use prefixes and suffixes to help you identify the meaning of a word and look for clues that the context and structure of the sentence give you.

Answer: E (merged)

 Some questions might ask you for the meaning of **more than one word** in the sentence. Remember to answer both parts of the question. It can be helpful to answer the part of the question that you find easier first.

 Read each sentence and then answer the questions that follow.

The spy's efforts to evade his captors proved futile.

1. What does 'futile' mean?

- **A.** succeed
- **B.** useless
- **C.** exhilarating
- **D.** interrogation
- **E.** enjoyable

Answer: _____

Her speech alluded to her promotion but did not dwell on the subject.

2. What does 'alluded' mean?

- **A.** glorified
- **B.** disagreed
- **C.** remarkable
- **D.** referred
- **E.** congratulating

Answer: _____

"You may have shown remorse for your actions but society cannot condone this crime," the judge rumbled.

3. What does 'remorse' mean?

- **A.** vanity
- **B.** apologise
- **C.** regret
- **D.** shameful
- **E.** consideration

Answer: _____

4. What does 'condone' mean?

- **A.** accept
- **B.** forbid
- **C.** illegal
- **D.** arrest
- **E.** wittingly

Answer: _____

These questions test your vocabulary by asking you to **sort** words into groups. You might have to identify what links a group of words or you might be told the link and have to group the words.

A	B	C	D
oboe	strawberry	finger	melancholy
clarinet	cherry	knee	frustration
bassoon	tomato	neck	joy
flute	raspberry	ankle	disappointment

Look at the words below. Which group in the table (**A**, **B**, **C** or **D**) does each of them belong to? Choose the correct letter and write it on the line.

i) nose ____

ii) shame ____

iii) recorder ____

iv) apple ____

v) excitement ____

vi) shin ____

First, identify the link between the words in each group in the table. Think about what the words have in common. You may be able to think of several connections between the words.

Then put the words in the question into the correct group.

Answer:

i) nose ___C___ *part of the body*

ii) shame ___D___ *emotion*

iii) recorder ___A___ *type of wind instrument*

iv) apple ___B___ *type of fruit*

v) excitement ___D___ *emotion*

vi) shin ___C___ *part of the body*

 Now answer the following questions.

1.

A	B	C	D
sloth	nickel	pistachio	mosquito
otter	gold	walnut	termite
wombat	zinc	cashew	louse
mongoose	copper	almond	cricket

Look at the words below. Which group in the table (**A**, **B**, **C** or **D**) does each of them belong to? Choose the correct letter and write it on the line.

i) pecan ____

ii) ape ____

iii) cockroach ____

iv) lead ____

v) flea ____

vi) acorn ____

Sort words into groups

For each question below, choose the word (**A**, **B**, **C**, **D** or **E**) that goes best with the words in brackets.

2. (galaxy, cluster, nebula)

  A. constellation   **B.** solar   **C.** astronaut   **D.** launch   **E.** terrestrial   ____

3. (cutlass, rapier, dagger)

  A. quiver   **B.** missile   **C.** kilt   **D.** sabre   **E.** svelte   ____

Sometimes, you will be given a link and you must categorise words according to this link.

Put the words below into the correct groups.

spatula   staple   violet   colander   magnolia   carnation   whisk   quill   envelope

Flowers	Cooking utensils	Stationery

This question relies on you knowing the meaning of these words. The wider your vocabulary, the more likely you are to be able to answer the question. If you are unsure of any of the meanings, start by grouping any words that you do recognise. Lightly cross them out when you have categorised them. You can then see how many gaps you have left to fill in each group and which words you have to choose from, which will help you make an educated guess.

Answer:

Flowers	Cooking utensils	Stationery
carnation	spatula	staple
violet	whisk	quill
magnolia	colander	envelope

 Now answer the following question.

4. Put the words below into the correct groups.

toboggan   rickshaw   charity   pleasure   glider   confusion   cider   soda   cordial

Abstract nouns	Beverages	Modes of transport

Ordering words

This question type requires you to order words according to their meaning. You will be given a set of words that you must arrange in sequence. You must think about how the words could relate to one another in terms of size and order them according to the instructions.

Put these words in sequence from smallest to largest, then identify the word in the middle.

spider   cat   millipede   snake   beetle

Think about how these words could relate to each other in terms of size. There may be more than one connection between them, so make sure you consider all the possibilities.

The words could relate to each other in terms of the physical size of the animals. A cat is usually bigger than a centipede, for example. However, a snake could be a small adder or a huge boa constrictor! Since it would be tricky to order these animals in terms of their physical size, you should look for another connection between the words.

The words could be ordered by the number of legs each creature has. A spider has eight, a cat has four, a millipede has at least 40, a snake has zero and a beetle has six.

The order of the words from smallest to largest would therefore be:

snake   cat   beetle   spider   millipede

Now the words are in order, you must identify the word in the middle.

snake   cat   (beetle)   spider   millipede

Answer: beetle

> (!) Although the words in this example are not orderable by physical size, many questions that you encounter could require you to order the words in this way. Always consider all the possible connections between the words you are given.

> (!) If you are asked to order emotions, order them according to their intensity. For example, **content** would come before **elated** in a sequence of smallest to largest.

Put these words in sequence from smallest to largest, then identify the word in the middle.

1. lake   droplet   pond   ocean   puddle   _____

2. hexagon   parallelogram   circle   pentagon   triangle   _____

3. fascinated   interested   bored   obsessed   ambivalent   _____

4. village   country   town   continent   city   _____

5. gram   tonne   milligram   kilogram   centigram   _____

6. vulture   gerbil   midge   rhinoceros   starling   _____

Schofield & Sims

Synonyms

Synonyms are words with similar meanings. Synonym questions test your understanding of word meanings and word type. There are several different types of synonym questions.

Words of a similar meaning

Underline the **two** words, **one** from each group, that are most similar in meaning.

(hot cool heat)   (oven ice cold)

First, **scan** the words. The answer may be obvious. If it is not, compare each word in the first set to each word in the second set. Work through the words in turn.

- Are **hot** and **oven** similar in meaning?   No.
- Are **hot** and **ice** similar in meaning?   No.
- Are **hot** and **cold** similar in meaning?   No.
- Are **cool** and **oven** similar in meaning?   No.
- Are **cool** and **ice** similar in meaning?   Yes.
- Are **cool** and **cold** similar in meaning?   Yes. They are more similar in meaning than **cool** and **ice**.

Answer: (hot <u>cool</u> heat)   (oven ice <u>cold</u>)

 Underline the **two** words, **one** from each group, that are most similar in meaning.

1. (almost always never)   (sometimes nearly now)

2. (repeat reply redo)   (undo answer refuse)

3. (sturdy detail fragile)   (delicate broken grand)

4. (essential essence easy)   (hard important difficult)

5. (diminish dessert disaster)   (leave reduce increase)

6. (strong weak week)   (small frail month)

7. (sweet sour batter)   (bitter lemon arrive)

8. (free compliment complex)   (flatter argue ignore)

 TIP If you are unsure, try putting each word into a sentence. For example, 'I **almost** won the race.' / 'I **nearly** won the race.' If the meaning stays the same, your choice is correct.

Synonyms

Words of a similar type or meaning

Some questions may contain words of a similar type rather than words that are similar in meaning.

Underline the **two** words that are of a similar type or meaning.

apple   mouse   pigeon   pear   green

Compare each word in turn with each of the other words. Think about the meaning. Decide whether the two words have any connections.

- Is **apple** similar to **mouse**?   No.
- Is **apple** similar to **pigeon**?   No.
- Is **apple** similar to **pear**?   Yes – they are both types of fruit. The two words are not similar in meaning, but they are of a similar type.

When you think you have found the answer, continue checking the other words. There might be a pair that is more closely connected.

- Is **apple** similar to **green**?   No.

Answer: <u>apple</u>   mouse   pigeon   <u>pear</u>   green

(!) These questions are laid out differently from the synonym questions on page 37. Here, you compare each word in turn with **all** the other words given, not just with those in a second group. Watch out for different question types and read the question carefully.

 Underline the **two** words in each line that are of a similar type or meaning.

9. ask   talk   reply   annoy   question

10. blame   defeat   assure   beat   lose

11. hound   feline   artistic   sneaky   crafty

12. destiny   detour   aloud   fate   fete

13. class   firm   soft   busy   engaged

14. intent   impolite   distress   rude   polite

15. bicycle   runway   station   bus   wing

16. lamp   kitchen   shed   carpet   bedroom

Schofield & Sims

Synonyms

Here are some other synonym question types you may encounter.

Underline the word in brackets that is closest in meaning to the word in capitals.

FURIOUS   (miserable, irritated, confused, irate, stressed)

Compare the meaning of the word in capitals to the meaning of each of the words in brackets until you find a word that has a similar meaning. Put a dot under it, then check the rest of the words to see if any other words have a similar meaning. Here, both **irritated** and **irate** have a similar meaning to **furious**, but **irate** represents a greater level of anger than **irritated**. **Irate** is therefore closer in meaning to **furious**, so it is the answer.

Answer: FURIOUS   (miserable, irritated, confused, <u>irate</u>, stressed)

 Underline the word in brackets that is closest in meaning to the word in capitals.

17. CREEP   (sneak, crawly, insect, scary, creak)

18. CAUTIOUS   (careful, warning, dangerous, anxious, undisturbed)

19. CONSEQUENCE   (final, outcome, important, alternate, conclude)

Sometimes, you will be given several pairs of words and will have to underline the pair of words that is most similar in meaning.

Underline the pair of words that is most similar in meaning.

high, low   anxiety, worried   push, shove

Starting with the first pair, think about what each word means and decide if they have a similar meaning. Ignore any other relationships between the words.

In this example, **high** and **low** are opposites so they are not the answer. **Anxiety** and **worry** do have a similar meaning, but they are not the same word class: **anxiety** is an abstract noun and **worried** is a verb. You can test them in a simple sentence to check. For example:

Sally was **worried** about the test. Sally was **anxiety** about the test.

The only pair left is **shove** and **push**. They do have a similar meaning and would both work in a simple sentence. For example:

Sally gave Robin a **push**. Sally gave Robin a **shove**. So, 'push, shove' is the answer.

Answer: high, low   anxiety, worried   <u>push</u>, <u>shove</u>

 Underline the pair of words that is most similar in meaning.

20. hazard, warning   clear, clean   positive, certain

21. shock, electric   health, ill   tremble, shake

22. intend, intense   criticise, denounce   weak, week

Synonyms

Sometimes, you may be given a word and asked to find a word that is similar in meaning that also rhymes with another given word.

Find the word that is similar in meaning to the word in capitals and that rhymes with the word in italics.

DRAW   *fetch*   _____

Think about synonyms of the word in capitals and check if they rhyme with the word in italics.

If the answer is not obvious at first, you could run through the alphabet to see if you can think of any words that rhyme with **fetch**. As you do, think about the meaning of the words and whether or not it is similar to **draw**. However, remember that the initial sound in the rhyming word may consist of several letters. In this example, the answer is **sketch** so the **f** has been replaced with **sk**. Also remember that the word in italics may have more than one pronunciation.

Answer: sketch

Find the word that is similar in meaning to the word in capitals and that rhymes with the word in italics.

23.   BEVERAGE   *sink*   _____

25.   RETRIEVE   *wind*   _____

24.   ESCAPE   *tree*   _____

Sometimes, you may need to add missing letters to complete a word so that it is similar in meaning to another given word.

Add the missing letters to make a word that is similar in meaning to the word in capitals.

INTELLIGENT   c __ __ v e __

Think about the meaning of the word in capitals and see if you can come up with any synonyms. As you do, check to see if the word contains the letters shown in the word on the right.

If you are struggling to come up with an answer, you could use your knowledge of vowels and spelling strings to help you. In the example above, the last letter is missing but the letter before it is **e**. Think about which letters are most likely to be on the end. Words often end in **–er** or **–ed** so you could try these out first. Also, there needs to be at least one vowel in between the **c** and **v**, but as the word starts with a **c** it is most likely that the first missing letter will be a consonant and the second one a vowel (because two vowels after a **c** is unusual). Think about the letters that commonly follow a **c** and try out various combinations in the spaces.

When you think you have found the answer, test it out by writing the missing letters into the gaps to see if they fit and if the word is spelt correctly. Write the letters faintly at first so you can rub them out if you realise you have made a mistake.

Answer: clever

Add the missing letters to make a word that is similar in meaning to the word in capitals.

26.   AMIABLE   fr __ __ n __ l __

28.   COSTLY   e __ pen __ i __ __

27.   PENSIVE   th __ __ __ __ t f __ __

Antonyms

Antonyms are words that are opposite in meaning. Antonym questions test your understanding of word meanings. Just like synonym questions, they may be presented in several different ways.

Choosing one word from each of two groups

Underline the **two** words, **one** from each group, that are most opposite in meaning.

(under enter over)   (around exit below)

Scan the words. The answer may be obvious. If it is not, compare each word in the first set to each word in the second set in turn:

- Are **under** and **around** opposites?   No.
- Are **under** and **exit** opposites?   No.
- Are **under** and **below** opposites?   No.
- Are **enter** and **around** opposites?   No.
- Are **enter** and **exit** opposites?   Yes.

Answer: (under <u>enter</u> over)   (around <u>exit</u> below)

 These questions look like **synonym** questions. Read them carefully. Make sure you look for words that are **opposite** in meaning.

 Underline the **two** words, **one** from each group, that are most opposite in meaning.

1.   (begin after stop)   (lend land end)

2.   (danger despair desperate)   (risk hope fear)

3.   (mean dark poor)   (dim dreary kind)

4.   (find full fast)   (empty quick found)

5.   (healthy include inside)   (hungry interior exclude)

6.   (movie genuine genius)   (real fake film)

7.   (perfect pendant new)   (brand antique perform)

8.   (accept letter gift)   (receive thank reject)

 To check your answer, put each word in a sentence. For example, 'I **always** eat my greens.' / 'I **never** eat my greens.' If swapping the words gives the sentence the opposite meaning, your answer is probably correct.

Choosing one pair of words from three given

Underline the pair of words that is most opposite in meaning.

(above, over)   (poppy, daffodil)   (large, small)

Starting with the first pair, think about what each word means and decide if they are opposite in meaning. It may help to visualise each word as an image or an action, comparing each one to its partner to see if they are opposites. Remember to ignore any other relationships between the words and think only about whether or not they have opposite meanings.

- **Above** and **over** have similar meanings.   Are they opposites? No.
- **Poppy** and **daffodil** are both types of flower.   Are they opposites? No.
- **Large** and **small** are both describing words.   Are they opposites? Yes.

Answer: (above, over)   (poppy, daffodil)   (<u>large</u>, <u>small</u>)

 Underline the pair of words that is most opposite in meaning.

9.   (better, superior)   (orange, banana)   (divulge, conceal)

10.   (maximum, minimum)   (loud, noisy)   (father, uncle)

11.   (beautiful, pretty)   (powerful, feeble)   (victory, vanity)

12.   (stretch, compress)   (merry, jolly)   (under, submerge)

 Underline one **pair** of words, **not** two **separate** words.

TIP If you are unsure of some word meanings, rule out the answers you know are wrong, then guess.

Choosing one word that is opposite to a single word given

Underline the **one** word inside the brackets that is most opposite in meaning to the word before the brackets.

cheap   (noisy, happy, expensive, bargain, shopping)

Think about the meaning of the word outside the brackets. Compare it in turn to each word inside the brackets. Think about the different meanings:

- Are **cheap** and **noisy** opposites?   No.
- Are **cheap** and **happy** opposites?   No.
- Are **cheap** and **expensive** opposites?   Yes.

Answer: cheap   (noisy, happy, <u>expensive</u>, bargain, shopping)

Underline the **one** word inside the brackets that is most opposite in meaning to the word before the brackets.

13. KNOWLEDGE   (wisdom, lazy, legal, question, ignorance)

14. HINDER   (hamper, annoy, help, hind, honest)

15. ENCOURAGE   (enthusiastic, bored, praise, discourage, disagree)

16. CURIOUS   (chaos, wonder, learn, indifferent, understand)

Here are some other antonym question types you may encounter.

Find the word that is opposite in meaning to the word in capitals and that rhymes with the word in italics.

UP   *crown*   _____

Think about the meaning of the word in capitals and run through any opposites in your head. Check if any of these words rhymes with **crown**. If the answer is not obvious at first, you could run through the alphabet to see if you can think of any words that rhyme with **crown**. As you do, think about the meaning of the words and whether or not it is opposite to **UP**. This may help you to think of the word. However, remember that the initial sound in the rhyming word may consist of several letters, so it is not simply a case of trying out each letter of the alphabet in turn. In this example, the answer is **down** so the **cr** has been replaced with **d**.

Also remember that the word in italics may have more than one pronunciation and that the answer may not follow the same spelling pattern.

Answer: down

 Find the word that is opposite in meaning to the word in capitals and that rhymes with the word in italics.

17. CROOKED   *weight*   _____

18. VICTORY   *moss*   _____

19. SAGE   *pool*   _____

20. COMMONPLACE   *spare*   _____

Add the missing letters to make a word that is opposite in meaning to the word in capitals.

LEND   b __ __ r o __

Think about the meaning of the word in capitals and see if you can come up with any opposites. As you do, check to see if the word contains the letters shown in the word on the right. When you think you have found the answer, test it out by writing the missing letters into the gaps to see if they fit and if the word is spelt correctly. Write the letters faintly at first so you can rub them out if you realise you have made a mistake.

If you are struggling to come up with an answer, you could use your knowledge of vowels and spelling strings to help you. In the example above, the last letter is missing but the letter before it is **o**. Think about which letters are most likely to be on the end. Common letters that follow **o** at the end of a word are **t**, **w**, **y** so you could try these out first. Also, there needs to be at least one vowel in between the **b** and **r** and it is also likely that there is a double **r** so try out the different vowels followed by a double **r** to see what you come up with.

When you think you have found the answer, write the missing letters faintly in the gaps and check that the word is opposite in meaning to the word in capitals. Once you are happy with your answer, write it in properly.

Answer: borrow

 Add the missing letters to make a word that is opposite in meaning to the word in capitals.

21. VAIN   __ o d __ __ t

22. CONSTRUCT   d __ s __ r o __

23. TEDIOUS   i __ t e r __ __ t __ __ g

24. MANUAL   a u __ __ m __ t __ d

Synonym and antonym grids

In these questions, you are given a grid containing a selection of words and you have to find synonyms, antonyms or both.

To tackle these question types, first read the question carefully and check what you have to find. If you are looking for synonyms, look at the given word and think of its meaning. Then scan each column of the grid in turn, comparing the given word to each word in the grid, thinking carefully about whether it is a synonym for that word. Use all the strategies you have used before. Once you have found a synonym, write the word down and then lightly cross it out in the grid.

The strategies for finding antonyms are the same: just make sure you always check carefully that you have found the correct words, as it is very easy to get muddled up and find antonyms rather than synonyms and vice versa.

 Use the grid to answer the questions below.

1.

pending	solution	lacklustre	cleanse	contrived
split	genuine	excel	merge	assertive
sorted	separate	healthy	unsettled	pollute
false	metallic	contaminate	insure	natural
sincere	corrupt	resolved	artisan	outstanding

i)   Find **three** synonyms for the word 'unresolved'.

_____   _____   _____

ii)   Find **two** antonyms for the word 'amalgamate'.

_____   _____

iii) Find **two** synonyms for the word 'artificial'.

_____   _____

iv)   Find **three** antonyms for the word 'purify'.

_____   _____   _____

Analogies

An **analogy** is a comparison. In verbal reasoning analogy questions, you look for ways in which two words relate to one another. Then you find another two words that relate to each other in a similar way. The connection must be the same for both halves of the sentence.

Real-life connections

Underline the **two** words, **one** from each group, that complete the sentence in the best way.

Cow is to (field, fish, calf) as **pig** is to (snout, piglet, animal).

First, scan the words. The correct answer may be obvious. If it is not, read the options carefully and follow these steps.

Compare the first word (**cow**) to each of the choices in turn. Do the words relate to each other? If so, in what way?

- Are **cow** and **field** connected?   Yes – a **cow** lives in a field.

Look at the words in the second set. Is there a word relating to **pig** in the same way? No: move on to the next word.

- Are **cow** and **fish** connected?   No – move on to the next word.
- Are **cow** and **calf** connected?   Yes – a **calf** is a **baby cow**. Look to see if there is a word that relates to **pig** in the same way.

Each time you look at the second set of words, you look for a connection that is similar to one of the connections you have found in the first set.

- Are **pig** and **snout** connected?   Yes – but not in the same way as **cow** and **field** or **cow** and **calf**.
- Are **pig** and **piglet** connected?   Yes – a **piglet** is a **baby pig**. The words are connected in the same way as **cow** and **calf**.

Once you think you have found the answer, read the sentence carefully. Check that the same comparison is made in both halves. Then underline the two words.

Answer: Cow is to (field, fish, <u>calf</u>) as **pig** is to (snout, <u>piglet</u>, animal).

 Underline the **two** words, **one** from each group, that complete the sentence in the best way.

1. **Fish** is to (walk, run, swim) as **bird** is to (trot, fly, jump).

2. **Grass** is to (long, green, mow) as **sand** is to (warm, beach, yellow).

3. **Uncle** is to (old, son, aunt) as **sister** is to (mother, girl, brother).

4. **Eleven** is to (twelve, number, two) as **four** is to (seven, for, five).

5. **Teacher** is to (bank, park, school) as **mechanic** is to (car, garage, tip).

6. **Elephant** is to (large, hide, trunk) as **dog** is to (seek, tail, coat).

Schofield & Sims

Analogies

There are four types of analogy question: real-life connections, opposites, similar meanings and spelling connections. For examples of real-life connections, the most common question type, see page 46. Examples of opposites questions are given below. For examples of similar meanings and spelling connections questions, see page 48.

Opposites

Underline the **two** words, **one** from each group, that complete the sentence in the best way.

Contest is to (game, rugby, agree) as **light** is to (bulb, heavy, warm).

Scan the words. The answer may be obvious.

If it is not, compare the first word (**contest**) to **game**, **rugby** and **agree**.

- **contest – game** and **contest – rugby** makes you think of the meaning 'competition'.
- **contest – agree** reminds you that **contest** also means 'disagree'.

Now look at the second set of words.

- **light – bulb** makes you think of the meaning 'brightness'.
- **light – heavy** reminds you that **light** also means 'not heavy'.

An **opposites** connection works in both parts of the sentence. **Contest** is the opposite of **agree**. **Light** is the opposite of **heavy**.

Check again that the same comparison is made in both halves of the sentence.

Answer: Contest is to (game, rugby, <u>agree</u>) as **light** is to (bulb, <u>heavy</u>, warm).

 TIP Look out for words that have more than one meaning.

 Underline the **two** words, **one** from each group, that complete the sentence in the best way.

7. **Left** is to (leave, right, wrong) as **horizontal** is to (sun, across, vertical).

8. **Attack** is to (fight, win, defend) as **expand** is to (extinct, contract, explain).

9. **Fresh** is to (stale, edible, air) as **humble** is to (old, pie, proud).

10. **Rush** is to (dawdle, jog, skip) as **adequate** is to (inadequate, less, quad).

11. **Clear** is to (wash, cloudy, simple) as **late** is to (eight, cup, early).

12. **Reward** is to (penalty, restore, revoke) as **relevant** is to (expect, recent, meaningless).

Similar meanings

With similar meanings analogies, look for the two words that are closest in meaning.

> Underline the **two** words, **one** from each group, that complete the sentence in the best way.
>
> **Prompt** is to (punctual, stage, prom) as **immeasurable** is to (limited, countless, ruler).

Scan the words. If the answer is not obvious, work through the options.

- The word **prompt** has connections with **punctual**, **stage** and **prom**.
- Only **one** of these connections is the same in both halves.
- **Prompt** and **punctual** have similar meanings. **Immeasurable** and **countless** have similar meanings.

Answer: Prompt is to (<u>punctual</u>, stage, prom) as **immeasurable** is to (limited, <u>countless</u>, ruler).

Spelling connections

These connections focus on letters, not meaning. There are three question types. The words in each pair may:

- be **homophones**

For example: **sea** is to (water, <u>see</u>, boat) as **sent** is to (parcel, spent, <u>scent</u>)

- be made by adding or removing a letter

For example: **port** is to (<u>pot</u>, ferry, wine) as **bear** is to (beer, <u>bar</u>, spider)

- have the same letters but in a different order

For example: **draw** is to (well, drawer, <u>ward</u>) as **rate** is to (race, <u>tear</u>, opinion)

 Underline the **two** words, **one** from each group, that complete the sentence in the best way.

13. **Main** is to (horse, mane, least) as **sight** is to (picture, taste, site).

14. **Gardener** is to (plants, grow, spade) as **painter** is to (artist, brush, colour).

15. **Stag** is to (deer, doe, antlers) as **bull** is to (horns, calf, field).

16. **Taps** is to (tops, money, spat) as **dab** is to (dot, bad, dip).

17. **Tree** is to (trunk, twigs, roots) as **building** is to (flat, foundations, home).

18. **Challenge** is to (succeed, finish, dare) as **implore** is to (improve, endure, beseech).

 TIP Remember the analogy types: similar meanings, opposites, real-life connections, spelling connections. Scan for an answer. Then work through each possibility.

Odd ones out

Odd ones out questions test your understanding of word meaning. You are given five words. You have to find the two words that do not go with the other three.

Underline the **two** words that are different from the other three.

giraffe   horse   octopus   cow   eel

First, find the three words that go together.

Look at each word in turn. Compare it to each of the others. Find what the words have in common.

- Are **giraffe** and **horse** connected?   Yes – both are animals with four legs and both are mammals.
- Are **giraffe** and **octopus** connected?   No.
- Are **giraffe** and **cow** connected?   Yes – both are animals with four legs and both are mammals.
- Are **giraffe** and **eel** connected?   No.

Therefore, **giraffe**, **horse** and **cow** are the three words that go together.

The two words that are different are **octopus** and **eel**.

Answer: giraffe   horse   <u>octopus</u>   cow   <u>eel</u>

 Underline the **two** words in each group that are different from the other three.

1. rose   mosquito   daffodil   cricket   tulip

2. mechanic   accountant   organ   solicitor   guitar

3. delight   dismay   joy   despair   misery

4. glider   helicopter   airship   yacht   canoe

5. mole   owl   badger   fox   kestrel

6. apple   lettuce   mango   salad   kiwi

7. betrayal   obedience   treachery   disloyalty   faith

8. first   second   gram   hour   year

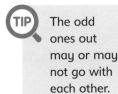
TIP The odd ones out may or may not go with each other.

These questions test your knowledge of words with more than one meaning.

Here are two pairs of words. Choose from the five possible answers on the left the **one** word that goes equally well with **both** the word pairs. Underline the word.

cost   good   fine   joyful   price   (fee, penalty)   (well, happy)

Read the words in brackets. Think about the meanings and how they are connected. Look at each of the five words in turn. Look for a connection with the word in brackets.

- Is **cost** connected with **fee, penalty**?   Yes – all are to do with paying money.
- Is **cost** connected with **well, happy**?   No.
- Is **good** connected with **fee, penalty**?   No.
- Is **fine** connected with **fee, penalty**?   Yes – all are to do with paying money.
- Is **fine** connected with **well, happy**?   Yes – all are to do with feeling good.

Answer: cost   good   <u>fine</u>   joyful   price

 TIP   Think of different pronunciations and meanings of the words. For example, **bow** can mean 'a knot with two loops' or 'to bend forward from the waist'. The meaning depends on the pronunciation.

   In the questions below, there are two pairs of words. Choose from the five possible answers on the left the **one** word that goes equally well with **both** the word pairs. Underline the word.

1.   boat   upset   row   swim   disagree   (paddle, propel)   (fight, argue)

2.   break   wail   sob   tear   spoil   (rip, cut)   (cry, weep)

3.   bruise   splint   spiral   revolve   wound   (injury, hurt)   (turned, twisted)

4.   doctor   ill   invalid   used   nurse   (patient, injured)   (defunct, obsolete)

5.   door   distant   close   conceal   hide   (shut, cover)   (near, almost)

6.   soil   sow   boar   grow   animal   (plant, cultivate)   (pig, hog)

7.   band   team   symbol   mark   class   (stripe, streak)   (group, squad)

8.   occasion   peach   anniversary   date   appeal   (fig, apricot)   (appointment, engagement)

Now test your skills with these practice pages. If you get stuck, go back to pages 32 to 50 for some reminders.

Word meanings

Read each sentence and then answer the questions that follow.

The astronaut's resolve to complete his training never faltered.

1. What does 'resolve' mean?

    A. determination

    B. record

    C. hesitation

    D. calculation

    E. decipher

    Answer: _____

The guests at the ball marvelled at their opulent surroundings.

2. What does 'opulent' mean?

    A. inelegant

    B. mediocre

    C. delirious

    D. fermented

    E. luxurious

    Answer: _____

Although the candidate was well qualified, he lacked charisma.

3. What does 'candidate' mean?

    A. edible

    B. applicant

    C. penitent

    D. suave

    E. aspiration

    Answer: _____

4. What does 'charisma' mean?

    A. accomplishments

    B. consistency

    C. outrage

    D. illusion

    E. personality

    Answer: _____

The affliction caused sufferers to grow emaciated rapidly.

5. What does 'affliction' mean?

    A. imprisonment

    B. compulsion

    C. disease

    D. caress

    E. stricture

    Answer: _____

6. What does 'emaciated' mean?

    A. crops

    B. concentrated

    C. curious

    D. skeletal

    E. renovated

    Answer: _____

Sort words into groups

1.

A	B	C	D
cinnamon	alabaster	iguana	cone
pepper	pearl	elephant	sphere
clove	cotton	lynx	cylinder
saffron	ivory	coyote	cuboid

Look at the words below. Which group in the table (**A**, **B**, **C** or **D**) does each of them belong to? Choose the correct letter and write it on the line.

i) prism ____

ii) cream ____

iii) cumin ____

iv) alligator ____

v) porcelain ____

vi) pyramid ____

2.

A	B	C	D
breadth	rose	dismayed	stew
volume	thistle	mournful	roast
perimeter	cactus	devastated	braise
area	holly	despondent	fry

Look at the words below. Which group in the table (**A**, **B**, **C** or **D**) does each of them belong to? Choose the correct letter and write it on the line.

i) wretched ____

ii) depth ____

iii) poach ____

iv) marinade ____

v) bramble ____

vi) desolate ____

For each question below, choose the word (**A**, **B**, **C**, **D** or **E**) that goes best with the words in brackets.

3. (consultation, dialogue, conference)

A. spoke   **B.** debate   **C.** conversion   **D.** relapse   **E.** victor   ____

4. (should, must, can)

A. probably   **B.** nought   **C.** might   **D.** willing   **E.** cleave   ____

5. Put the words below into the correct groups.

runes   hyphen   sarong   ellipsis   dungarees   leotard   colon   braille   hieroglyphs

Clothing	Writing systems	Punctuation marks

Schofield & Sims

Ordering words

Put these words in sequence from smallest to largest, then identify the word in the middle.

1. irked   tranquil   enraged   angry   incandescent   _____

2. blueberry   watermelon   satsuma   strawberry   artichoke   _____

3. motorbike   ski   lorry   unicycle   tricycle   _____

4. lifetime   fortnight   eon   decade   moment   _____

5. sunflower   moss   redwood   dandelion   oak   _____

6. gale   gust   hurricane   calm   breeze   _____

Synonyms

Underline the **two** words, **one** from each group, that are most similar in meaning.

7. (bargain question baffle)   (confuse price answer)

8. (thankful bold afraid)   (bald fearless praise)

Underline the **two** words in each line that are of a similar type or meaning.

9. dull   racket   sport   din   shiny   10. conflict   peace   part   feud   avoid

Underline the word in brackets that is closest in meaning to the word in capitals.

11. SERENE   (cerebral, superficial, severe, tranquil, angelic)

12. EXCEED   (extreme, ample, excellent, improve, surpass)

Underline the pair of words that is most similar in meaning.

13. ask, request   sting, bite   lose, loose

14. wonder, wander   erase, delete   kind, generous

Find the word that is similar in meaning to the word in capitals and that rhymes with the word in italics.

15. BATTLE *light* _____   16. ENDEAVOUR *fly* _____

Add the missing letters to make a word that is similar in meaning to the word in capitals.

17. VESSEL __ __ n t __ __ n e r   18. COURAGEOUS v __ l __ a __ __

Antonyms

Underline the **two** words, **one** from each group, that are most opposite in meaning.

1. (new ancient ancestor)   (modern moderate moreover)

2. (artificial arrange entrance)   (fake natural unkind)

Underline the pair of words that is most opposite in meaning.

3. (optimist, pessimist)   (doctor, nurse)   (enhance, boost)

4. (complex, simple)   (squeeze, crush)   (question, interrogate)

Underline the **one** word inside the brackets that is most opposite in meaning to the word before the brackets.

5. DISHEVELLED   (unkempt, tidy, uncertain, hopeful, level)

Find the word that is opposite in meaning to the word in capitals and that rhymes with the word in italics.

6. LENIENT   *picked*   _____

Add the missing letters to make a word that is opposite in meaning to the word in capitals.

7. UNSURE   c __ __ f __ d __ __ t

....

Synonym and antonym grids

8. Use the grid to answer the questions below.

rotten	blame	petty	game	explosive
tempestuous	fresh	serious	tranquil	clear
precise	deficient	decayed	critical	contaminate
crazy	stable	establish	unclear	joyful
insignificant	delighted	edible	unimportant	serene

i) Find **three** synonyms for the word 'trivial'.

_____   _____   _____

ii) Find **two** antonyms for the word 'vague'.

_____   _____

iii) Find **two** synonyms for the word 'putrid'.

_____   _____

iv) Find **three** antonyms for the word 'volatile'.

_____   _____   _____

Analogies

Underline the **two** words, **one** from each group, that complete the sentence in the best way.

1. **Over** is to (down, under, out) as **enter** is to (entrance, into, exit).

2. **Racket** is to (noise, badminton, cricket) as **stick** is to (tree, hockey, glue).

3. **Ball** is to (cry, bawl, bowl) as **seam** is to (seal, dress, seem).

4. **Fashion** is to (clothes, trend, model) as **bet** is to (wager, bat, win).

5. **Clarinet** is to (music, wind, play) as **drum** is to (percussion, sticks, loud).

6. **Apple** is to (fruit, red, pip) as **plum** is to (vegetable, juicy, stone).

7. **Leap** is to (pale, jump, high) as **rear** is to (rare, rhyme, steer).

8. **Hire** is to (recruit, lower, high) as **ability** is to (clever, aptitude, agility).

Odd ones out

Underline the **two** words in each group that are different from the other three.

9. birch   oak   acorn   flower   willow

10. school   college   church   university   temple

11. anger   fear   rage   fury   delight

12. increase   reduce   diminish   inflate   lessen

13. youth   doctor   infant   nurse   child

14. crib   sleep   bed   cot   dream

15. trout   salmon   seal   cod   dolphin

16. mother   brother   uncle   sister   wife

Word connections

In the questions below, there are two pairs of words. Choose from the five possible answers on the left the **one** word that goes equally well with **both** the word pairs. Underline the word.

17. money   church   change   repair   jottings   (coins, notes)   (alter, amend)

18. draft   twist   hurricane   wind   spin   (gale, breeze)   (turn, rotate)

19. subject   learn   hurt   expert   plan   (topic, lesson)   (inflict, expose)

20. toilet   waste   dress   sewer   haberdasher   (drain, effluent)   (seamstress, tailor)

21. sand   beach   sign   hand   wave   (sea, water)   (gesture, signal)

22. galaxy   planet   star   moon   hero   (sun, comet)   (famous, idol)

23. holdall   cause   support   case   pouch   (argument, defence)   (bag, cover)

24. leave   land   grass   stay   enter   (alight, arrive)   (ground, earth)

Singular and plural

These questions ask you to find the plural version of a word you are given. Most plurals are formed by adding **–s** to the end of the singular form of the word. However, some words with particular endings follow other rules, which you must learn. There are also irregular plurals that do not follow set rules, which you must learn separately.

Some questions may ask you to write in the correct plural.

> Complete the sentence, using the plural form of the word in brackets.
>
> Maisie listened to the _____ (echo) reverberate around the chamber.
>
> The plural of **echo** is formed by adding **–es** to make **echoes**. You must write the answer on the line, taking care with your spelling.
>
> **Answer:** Maisie listened to the _____**echoes**_____ (echo) reverberate around the chamber.

Some questions may ask you to identify the correct plural instead.

> Choose the correct plural to complete the sentence. Underline your answer.
>
> The *gooses* / *geese* / *geeses* pecked at the bread.
>
> The plural of **goose** is irregular – **geese**. You must underline the answer.
>
> **Answer:** The *gooses* / <u>*geese*</u> / *geeses* pecked at the bread.

✎ Complete each sentence, using the plural form of the word in brackets.

1. The detective struggled to identify the wily _____ (thief).

2. We are learning about famous scientific _____ (discovery) at school.

3. As she watched the _____ (video), she began to feel more optimistic.

4. All that was visible from the ridge was miles of desert dotted with _____ (cactus).

5. The full moon made him shiver as he remembered the old man's tale about the _____ (werewolf).

Choose the correct plural to complete the sentence. Underline your answer.

6. There are many competing *beliefs* / *believes* / *belieffs* about the existence of alien life.

7. The community guarded itself rigorously against possible *crisises* / *crisies* / *crises*.

8. He flicked the first of the *dominos* / *dominoes* / *dominose* and giggled as they began to tumble.

9. My plate was laden with succulent strawberries and velvety *peachs* / *peachies* / *peaches*.

10. The warrior's *loyalties* / *loyaltys* / *loyaltes* were divided when his son joined the enemy's ranks.

Root words, prefixes and suffixes

These questions test your recognition of root words and your use of prefixes and suffixes. You might be asked to identify the root of a word.

Find the roots of these words. Write each answer on the line.

disregarded _____   education _____

To help you to recognise the root, you can remove any prefixes or suffixes from the word you are given. If you remove **dis–** (a prefix meaning 'not') and **–ed** (a suffix which changes a verb into the past tense) from **disregarded**, you are left with the root word **regard**.

Understanding the meaning and function of particular prefixes and suffixes is very useful. **–ion** is a suffix which changes a verb into a noun. Knowing this, it is possible to see that **education** is the noun formed from the verb **educate**.

Answer: disregarded _____**regard**_____   education _____**educate**_____

You may also be asked to add a prefix or suffix to a root word to make it fit the context of a sentence.

Add the correct prefix or suffix to complete the sentence in the best way.

The venom __ __ __ snake slithered through the grass.

Begin by reading the whole sentence. You may find that your brain naturally fills the gap to make the sentence make sense. If it does not, think more carefully about which word is needed to fill the gap. It is likely to be an adjective. Which three-letter suffix could change the root word **venom** into an adjective?

The suffix **–ous** would fit the gap. It means 'full of' and changes a noun into an adjective. Check that the sentence would make sense if you added this suffix: 'The venomous snake slithered through the grass.' This sentence does make sense, so **–ous** is the answer. Write it in the gap.

Answer: The venom _o_ _u_ _s_ snake slithered through the grass.

Find the roots of these words. Write each answer on the line.

1. purify   _____

2. disrespectful _____

3. misleading   _____

> (!) You might be asked to complete a sentence by adding a prefix or a suffix to a root word you are given in brackets.

Add the correct prefix or suffix to complete the sentence in the best way.

4. The family hoped that they would not suffer any __ __ __ fortune.

5. You are the _____ (hungry) person in the restaurant.

6. Dinner was delayed because the chef forgot to _____ (heat) the oven.

This type of question tests your knowledge of word classes and how words are used in a sentence. You may be asked to identify words that belong to a particular word class.

Underline the preposition in the sentence below.

The kitten hid under the blanket.

Answer: The kitten hid <u>under</u> the blanket.

A preposition is a word that shows the connection between a noun or pronoun and another word or part of a sentence. Prepositions show where, when or how something happens. In this sentence, **under** is the preposition.

You may also be asked to sort all the words in a sentence according to their word class.

Complete the table using words from the sentence below.

Jerome, a keen traveller, desperately wanted to visit Australia but unfortunately he was afraid of spiders.

Adjective		
Adverb		
Verb		
Common noun		
Proper noun		

Look at the table to see which word classes you need to identify. Read the sentence, looking for each word class in turn. It may help to start with the proper nouns as these always start with capital letters. In this example sentence, the words **Jerome** and **Australia** are proper nouns. Then identify the common nouns – remember these can be people, places or things. In this example, the words **spiders** and **traveller** are common nouns. Adjectives describe nouns so, once you have identified the nouns, it is easier to spot the adjectives. In this sentence, the adjectives are **keen** and **afraid** (both words describing the traveller). Verbs are action words, so in this sentence the words **wanted** and **visit** are the verbs. Adverbs modify (or add more information to) verbs, adjectives or other adverbs and are often used to show degree, attitude, place or time. In this sentence, the adverbs are **desperately** and **unfortunately** (both describing attitudes).

Answer:

Adjective	keen	afraid
Adverb	desperately	unfortunately
Verb	wanted	visit
Common noun	traveller	spiders
Proper noun	Jerome	Australia

 TIP Words can change class depending on how they are used in a sentence. For instance, **fish** is a noun in the sentence 'She caught a fish', but a verb in the sentence 'We will fish tomorrow'.

Word classes

Some questions may ask you to identify the correct verb or **connective** to complete a sentence. Use the context of the sentence to help you. Think about the tense of verbs and the purpose of connectives.

> The sentence below contains a verb that has been used incorrectly. Rewrite the sentence using the correct form of the verb.
>
> I holding my little brother's hand on our way to school yesterday.
>
> The action is happening in the past, so **holding** needs to be changed to **held**.
>
> **Answer:** I **held** my little brother's hand on our way to school yesterday.

 Now answer the following questions.

 Rather than rewriting the sentence, you may be asked to choose the correct form of a verb to complete the sentence.

1. Underline the pronoun in the sentence below.

   The teacher congratulated me for winning the prize.

2. Complete the table using words from the sentence below.

   Jenny is the loudest singer in the choir, Annabel thought to herself, and definitely the least tuneful.

Adjective		
Adverb		
Verb		
Common noun		
Proper noun		

3. The sentence below contains a verb that has been used incorrectly. Rewrite the sentence on the line using the correct form of the verb.

   After I have finished ate this piece of cherry cake, I will wash my hands.

   _____

   _____

4. Circle the correct form of the verb in the sentence below.

   Thalia had   driving / driven / drove   around the neighbourhood several times.

Circle the connective that completes each sentence below in the best way.

5. Eoin must practise for his driving test   otherwise / although / before   he might fail.

6. All the children had chocolate ice-cream for dessert   yet / except / moreover   Priti, who felt nauseous.

Word tenses

This type of question tests your knowledge of verb tenses. You may be asked to rewrite a sentence you are given in the past tense.

Rewrite the sentence below using the past tense.

Jotham shouts at the television.

The verb in the sentence is **shouts**. To change it into the past tense you remove the **–s** and add **–ed** instead.

Answer: Jotham shouted at the television.

(!) Remember that some verbs are irregular – you must learn how different verbs are turned into the past tense in order to answer these questions.

Sometimes, you may have to write the correct tense of a verb to complete a sentence.

Write the correct tense of the verb in brackets to complete this sentence.

The race is _____ (start) soon.

The context of the sentence indicates what tense is needed. **Soon** shows that the race has not happened yet, and the use of the word **is** shows the sentence is in the present continuous tense. The answer is therefore **starting**.

Answer: The race is _____**starting**_____ (start) soon.

Rewrite the sentences below using the past tense.

1. Anisa draws in her sketchbook.

    _____

2. The student speaks to the professor.

    _____

3. He runs an errand for his parents and then does his homework.

    _____

Write the correct tense of the verb in brackets to complete each sentence.

4. Your aunt is _____ (hope) to receive a letter from you soon.

5. The surgeon did all he _____ (can) to save the patient.

6. The athlete had not _____ (beat) the record yet.

Now test your skills with these practice pages. If you get stuck, go back to pages 56 to 60 for some reminders.

Singular and plural

Complete each sentence, using the plural form of the word in brackets.

1. The kitten covered her arms in _____ (scratch).

2. Gordon handed out the _____ (dictionary) to his classmates.

3. Alana shared her home-grown _____ (tomato) with her friends.

4. All the _____ (runner-up) were given certificates.

5. The bowl of _____ (cherry) looked delicious.

6. Sylvie gasped as the _____ (deer) loped past her.

Choose the correct plural to complete the sentence. Underline your answer.

7. Joe's mother put some new *shelfs / shelves* up in his bedroom.

8. The bear caught three *salmons / salmon*.

9. My grandmother told me she had many happy *memories / memorys* of her childhood.

10. I baked two delicious *loafs / loaves* of fresh bread.

11. Over one hundred *bicycles / bicycle* have been stolen from our station in the past year.

12. Three *roofs / roofes* were struck by lightning during the storm.

Root words, prefixes and suffixes

Find the roots of these words. Write each answer on the line.

13. unkindly _____

14. needless _____

15. immature _____

16. abnormality _____

17. uncomfortable _____

18. bicycle _____

Add the correct prefix or suffix to complete the sentence in the best way.

19. He was thank __ __ __ for her help with the situation.

20. I told my naughty dog not to _____ (obey) me again.

21. My sore foot gave me a major _____ (advantage) in the race.

22. Lara felt _____ (hope) that she might win the competition.

23. Dexter spoke _____ (polite) to the stranger.

24. Naomi joined a choir to help overcome her _____ (lonely).

Word classes

1.   Underline the connective in the sentence below.

It was raining heavily but we had to give the dogs a walk.

2.   Complete the table using words from the sentence below.

Recently, some determined scientists in America built a groundbreaking robot and carefully landed it on Mars.

Adjective		
Adverb		
Verb		
Common noun		
Proper noun		

3.   The sentence below contains a verb that has been used incorrectly. Rewrite the sentence on the line using the correct form of the verb.

Her colleague went ahead without waiting for her to making the decision.

_____

4.   Circle the correct form of the verb in the sentence below.

Lola   brung   /   brought   /   bought   her pet hamster to school today.

5.   Circle the connective that completes the sentence in the best way.

You must whisper the password   because   /   but   /   before   I will let you in.

Word tenses

Rewrite the sentences below using the past tense.

6.   My sister goes to the theatre to watch a ballet performance.

_____

7.   I will take my dog for a walk.

_____

Write the correct tense of the verb in brackets to complete each sentence.

8.   Last night Jamilia _____ (dream) that she was a world-famous cricketer.

9.   Shaun was _____ (begin) to understand the topic.

10.   Nadia will be _____ (prepare) dinner tonight.

Missing letter

In these questions, you are given a pair of words. A letter is missing from the end of the first word and the beginning of the second word. You have to find the one missing letter that completes both words.

Find the letter that will end the first word and start the second.

gra (____) agic

Look at the incomplete words. Say them in your head. The answer may come to you.

If it does not, go through the alphabet. Try each letter in turn. Add it to the end of the first word.

- gra (**a**) = graa   Is this a word?   No – move on to the next letter.

Once you have found a letter that spells a word, try the same letter at the beginning of the second word.

- gra (**b**) = grab   Is this a word?   Yes – try it with the second word.
- (**b**) agic = bagic   Is this a word?   No.

Work through the alphabet to find another letter that completes the first word. Try it with the second word. Repeat until you find a letter that completes both words.

- gra (**m**) = gram   Is this a word?   Yes – try it with the second word.
- (**m**) agic = magic   Is this a word?   Yes.

Answer: gra (**m**) agic

If you have no luck with the first word, work with the second word instead.

> (!) In multiple-choice tests you are given a choice of five letters. Try each letter in turn, as above.

Find the letter that will end the first word and start the second word.

1. spin (____) yes

2. strea (____) eat

3. gree (____) omb

4. sou (____) iglet

5. tow (____) eck

6. sof (____) pple

Sometimes, you are given two pairs of words, both with the same letter missing.

Find the **one** missing letter that will complete both pairs of words. It will end the words before the brackets and start the words after the brackets.

man (____) olk   buo (____) awn

The technique is the same as for one pair of words. However, once you have found a letter to complete the first pair you must try the same letter with the second pair too.

- man (**e**) = mane   Is this a word?   Yes – try it with the second word.
- (**e**) olk = eolk   Is this a word?   No – try a different letter with the first word.
- man (**y**) = many   Is this a word?   Yes – try it with the second word.
- (**y**) olk = yolk   Is this a word?   Yes – try it with the third word.
- buo (**y**) = buoy   Is this a word?   Yes – try it with the fourth word.
- (**y**) awn = yawn   Is this a word?   Yes.

Answer: man (**y**) olk
buo (**y**) awn

Missing letter

✎ Find the **one** missing letter that will complete both pairs of words.

7. wal (____) ing   mil (____) ite

8. cla (____) ine   lea (____) ound

9. wav (____) at   tim (____) arth

10. stin (____) nat   dra (____) lare

11. trai (____) ought   gri (____) ear

12. mil (____) ake   stea (____) ive

> **TIP** Say the different sounds that the letters can make. For example, vowel sounds can be long or short and some letters combine to make a new sound.

Sometimes, you may be given a pair of words with two letters missing. Both letters will finish the first word and begin the second word. You must work out what this pair of letters is.

Find **two** letters that will end the first word and begin the second word.

bee (____ ____) air

To solve these questions, use the same strategy as you did for single missing letters, only this time run through the possible two-letter combinations that could end the first word. When you think of a letter pair that makes a correctly spelt first word, see if those letters also work at the beginning of the second word. If you do not find an answer this way, you could try starting with the second word and running through all the possible letter combinations that could go at the beginning, then testing these out to see which, if any, work at the end of the first word.

- bee + ck = beeck   Is this a correct spelling?   No.
- bee + rd = beerd   Is this a correct spelling?   No.
- bee + st = beest   Is this a correct spelling?   No.
- bee + dy = beedy   Is this a correct spelling?   No.
- bee + ch = beech   Is this a correct spelling?   Yes, beech is a type of tree.
                          Does it work at the start of 'air'?   Yes.

Answer: bee (_c_ _h_) air

✎ Find **two** letters that will end the first word and begin the second word.

13. wai (____ ____) and

14. boun (____ ____) iling

15. vir (____ ____) age

16. tremb (____ ____) arn

17. gra (____ ____) end

18. maj (____ ____) gan

Move a letter

In these questions, you are given two words. You take a letter from the first word so that it leaves a correctly spelt word. You then put the same letter into the second word to make another word. The order of the letters cannot be changed.

Move **one** letter from the first word to the second word to make **two** new words. Write the new words on the lines.

first   tack   _____   _____

Look at the first word. Cover each letter in turn. Do the remaining letters make a real word?

- ~~f~~irst = irst   Is this a real word?   No.
- fi~~r~~st = fist   Is this a real word?   Yes.
- fi~~r~~st = frst   Is this a real word?   No.

Once you have made a real word, put the same letter in front of the first letter of the second word. Try it in every position in turn.

- rtack   Is this a real word?   No.
- track   Is this a real word?   Yes.

Answer: r moves, to make **fist** and **track**

Move **one** letter from the first word to the second word to make **two** new words. Write the new words on the lines.

1.   yearn   sail   :   ____   moves, to make

_____   and   _____

2.   brought   down   :   ____   moves, to make

_____   and   _____

3.   clamp   hill   :   ____   moves, to make

_____   and   _____

4.   trust   burn   :   ____   moves, to make

_____   and   _____

5.   brand   head   :   ____   moves, to make

_____   and   _____

6.   grain   bean   :   ____   moves, to make

_____   and   _____

> **TIP** If you find it difficult to imagine the new words, write them down. Then you will find them easier to check.

Word ladders

This question type tests your vocabulary and spelling ability. You are given two words and you must change the first word into the last word, changing one letter at a time. When you change a letter, the new word you create must be a real word. You might be asked to reach the final word via one 'stepping stone' word in the middle, or via two 'stepping stone' words.

Change the first word into the last word. Change only one letter at a time and make a new, different word in the middle.

CASK _____ TALK

Look at the words you have been given. Which letters in **CASK** need to change to make **TALK**? **C** must become **T** and **S** must become **L**.

When you have identified which letters must change, you must decide which letter should change first. Think about which letter in **CASK** could be changed to make a real word.

CASK → TASK   ✓ **TASK** is a real word.

CASK → CALK   ✗ **CALK** is not a real word.

Check that you have found the correct answer. You should be able to change the 'stepping stone' word into the final word by changing the remaining letter you identified earlier.

TASK → TALK   ✓ Changing **S** to **L** makes **TALK**.

Write the 'stepping stone' word on the line.

Answer: CASK   **TASK**   TALK

Change the first word into the last word. Change only one letter at a time and make a new, different word in the middle.

1. FEND _____ BEAD

2. LESS _____ LOSE

3. POUT _____ SOUR

4. GOAD _____ TOED

5. VOTE _____ HOLE

6. HELP _____ HEAR

> **!** 'Stepping stone' words cannot be proper nouns.

Word ladders

You may be asked to change the first word into the final word via two 'stepping stone' words. You can follow the same steps as before, but you will have to identify three letters that must be changed in order to make the final word.

Change the first word into the last word. Change only one letter at a time and make **two** new, different words in the middle.

DEAL _____ _____ FELT

Look at the words and identify which letters must change. **D** must become **F**, **A** must become **L** and **L** must become **T**.

Decide which letter must be changed first to make a new, real word.

DEAL → FEAL   ✗ **FEAL** is not a real word.

DEAL → DELL   ✓ **DELL** is a real word.

DEAL → DEAT   ✗ **DEAT** is not a real word.

The first 'stepping stone' word must be **DELL**.

DEAL _____**DELL**_____ _____ FELT

The letters left to be changed are **D** to **F** and **L** to **T**. Decide which letter must be changed next to make another new, real word.

DELL → FELL   ✓ **FELL** is a real word.

DELL → DELT   ✗ **DELT** is not a real word.

Check that you have found the correct answer. You should be able to change the second 'stepping stone' word into the final word by making the remaining letter change.

FELL → FELT   ✓ Changing **L** to **T** makes **FELT**.

Answer: DEAL _____**DELL**_____ _____**FELL**_____ FELT

Change the first word into the last word. Change only one letter at a time and make **two** new, different words in the middle.

7.   NAIL   _____ _____ HILL

8.   PURR   _____ _____ SIRE

9.   BASE   _____ _____ MALT

10. GUSH   _____ _____ DUCT

11. WICK   _____ _____ PACT

12. FILM   _____ _____ PALE

In these questions, you are given a sentence. One of the words in the sentence is shown in capitals. It has had three letters removed. These three letters are consecutive and spell a three-letter word. You have to give the word.

The word in capitals has had three letters next to each other taken out. These three letters make one correctly spelt word without changing the order. Write the word on the line.

It was an exciting football **CH**. _____

Read the sentence carefully. The answer may come to you.

If it does not, read the sentence again. Think of a word that would make sense. Does it contain the letters given?

It was an exciting football ...   **GAME**? No – doesn't contain **C** and **H**.   **MATCH**? Yes – contains **C** and **H**.

Write out the whole word, crossing out the letters given.

MAT~~CH~~   The missing three letters spell **MAT**.   **Answer: MAT**

✎ The word or letter in capitals has had three letters next to each other taken out. These three letters make one correctly spelt word without changing the order. Write the word on the line.

1.   Would you like this cake or **T** one?   _____

2.   I went to **VI** my grandmother in hospital.   _____

3.   I **SPED** over on the ice.   _____

4.   My little sister **WS** a doll for her birthday.   _____

5.   **W** do you get your exam results?   _____

TIP Before you write the answer, write the longer word in full to make sure the spelling looks correct.

Sometimes, you might be asked to find three missing letters to complete words. In these questions, the three missing letters do not have to make a word.

Find the **three** letters that complete these words.   **Answer: ell** (marvellous)

marv __ __ __ ous   fan __ __ __ tic   **tas** (fantastic)

✎ Find the **three** letters that complete these words.

6.   ill __ __ __ rate   rec __ __ __ end   **9.**   tho __ __ __ tful   cons __ __ __ rate

7.   un __ __ __ al   en __ __ __ tain   **10.**   unex __ __ __ ted   oc __ __ __ ional

8.   reb __ __ __ ion   incre __ __ __ le

If you are doing a multiple-choice test, you are given five three-letter words to choose from. Try each possible answer with the letters given.

The boy jumped out and **SED** his little sister.

Answers

HAT	☐
ROD	☐
CAR	☐
PEN	☐
SHE	☐

Read the sentence. Look at the answers given. The answer may come to you.

If it does not, look at the word with the missing letters. Decide where the letters may have been taken from, then try them out.

ED often comes at the end of a word. So, the missing letters are either at the beginning or after the **S**. First, try each answer at the start of the word.

HATSED   **RODSED**   **CARSED**   **PENSED**   **SHESED**   None of these are real words.

Next, try each answer after the **S**.

SHATED   **SRODED**   **SCARED**   Answer option C (CAR) makes SCARED. This is a real word.

Check that your chosen word makes sense in the sentence.

The boy jumped out and **SCARED** his little sister.

Answer: CAR

 The word in capitals has had three letters next to each other taken out. These three letters make one correctly spelt word without changing the order. Find the word. Mark it with a **horizontal** line like this ▬ in the answer box.

11. My dad went into **HOSAL** for an operation.

12. The old lady was **ALED** by the tragic news.

13. You need to press the 'on' **SCH** to make it work.

11.

PUT	☐
MOP	☐
ARE	☐
LEG	☐
PIT	☐

12.

DOG	☐
ARM	☐
ROW	☐
PEN	☐
SUN	☐

13.

WIT	☐
RIP	☐
CAT	☐
DIG	☐
LOW	☐

This question type tests your spelling skills and attention to detail. You may be asked to identify a word that can be spelt using the letters of another word or a set of letters you are given. However, you must read the question carefully as you may also be asked to find the word which cannot be spelt using the letters given.

Underline the only word that **can** be made using the letters of the word on the left.

F O R E S T R Y   ferret   error   truer   fresh   oyster

To answer this question, first lightly cross out any answer that contains letters which the word on the left does not. There is no **u** or **h** in **FORESTRY**, so you can eliminate **truer** and **fresh**.

Then work carefully through the remaining answers and compare each one, letter by letter, to the word on the left. Tick each letter that appears in both the word on the left and the answer you are considering. As soon as you reach a letter that does not appear in the word on the left, you know that this cannot be the answer.

F O R E S T R Y   ferret   error   ~~truer~~   ~~fresh~~   oyster

f e r r e t   e r r o r   o y s t e r
✓✓✓✗✓   ✓✓✓✓✗   ✓✓✓✓✓✓

The answer is **oyster** as it is the only word which is spelt using just the letters found in **FORESTRY**.

Answer: ferret   error   truer   fresh   <u>oyster</u>

 If a letter appears twice in one of the answers, it must also appear twice in the word on the left. For instance, **e** appears twice in the word **ferret** but only once in **FORESTRY**, therefore **ferret** cannot be the answer.

 If you are asked which word **cannot** be spelt using the letters in the word on the left, use the same process, ticking the letters that appear in both the word on the left and the possible answer. You will find that all of the possible answers are spelt using the letters of the word on the left except for one. This one word will be your answer.

You may be given a group of letters rather than a word and be asked to identify which is the only word that can or cannot be made using them.

Underline the only word that **cannot** be made using the letters on the left.

i a t h r l   liar   hail   hair   real   trial

Follow the same method as before to identify the one word that is not made using only the letters on the left.

Answer: liar   hail   hair   <u>real</u>   trial

Words with letters in common

You may be asked to identify words in a group that are spelt using the same letters.

Circle the **two** words that are spelt using the same letters.

END   TON   TOE   TEN   NOT

Compare each of the words carefully. Look for letters that either appear in only **one** of the words or that appear in **all but one** of the words. Lightly cross out any of these words. Keep comparing the remaining words as you work through eliminating answers.

END is the only word that contains the letter **D** so it cannot be the answer.

~~END~~   TON   TOE   TEN   NOT

With **END** eliminated, **TEN** is now the only word that does not contain the letter **O**. Since it is missing this letter, it cannot be spelt using the same letters as any of the other words in the group. Therefore **TEN** can also be eliminated.

~~END~~   TON   TOE   ~~TEN~~   NOT

Out of the remaining words, **TOE** is now the only word that contains the letter **E**. Therefore, **TOE** cannot be the answer. This leaves **TON** and **NOT** as the answer, as these are the only two words that are spelt using the same letters.

~~END~~   TON   ~~TOE~~   ~~TEN~~   NOT

Answer: END   (TON)   TOE   TEN   (NOT)

> **TIP** If eliminating answers leaves you with more than two words remaining, carefully compare one word at a time to the others. Look out for differences between them, especially for letters that appear more than once in a word; they may not appear the same number of times in the word you are comparing.

 Underline the only word that **can** be made using the letters of the word on the left.

1.   A N A L O G U E   glued   agile   lunge   dangle   longer

2.   S W A M P E D   dampen   mapped   waves   dames   aimed

Underline the only word that **cannot** be made using the letters of the word on the left.

3.   R E I M A G I N E   mirage   engine   agree   aiming   genre

4.   P A R R O T E D   order   depart   report   drape   topped

Underline the only word that **can** be made using the letters on the left.

5.   d e r a f i n   neared   drained   derail   friend   finger

Underline the only word that **cannot** be made using the letters on the left.

6.   s n a u d h t o   shouts   dust   south   haunts   toads

In each group of words below, circle the **two** words that are spelt using the same letters.

7.   DAB   BUS   BED   BAD   DUB   8.   CLAP   YELP   LACY   PLAY   CLAY

Spot the word

In these questions, you are given a sentence. There is a four-letter word hidden at the end of one word and the beginning of the next. You have to find the hidden word.

Find the hidden four-letter word in the sentence below. Underline the word and write it on the line.

I wonder how she did in her maths test.   _____

Read the sentence carefully. The answer may be obvious. If it is not, go through the sentence. Look at the end of each word and the beginning of the next. It may help to cover the other letters so that you only see four letters at once. Carry on until you spot a four-letter word.

I wonder how she did in her maths test.	Is iwon a word?	No.
I wonder how she did in her maths test.	Is derh a word?	No.
I wonder how she did in her maths test.	Is erho a word?	No.
I wonder how she did in her maths test.	Is rhow a word?	No.
I wonder how she did in her maths test.	Is hows a word?	No.
I wonder how she did in her maths test.	Is owsh a word?	No.
I wonder how she did in her maths test.	Is wshe a word?	No.
I wonder how she did in her maths test.	Is shed a word?	Yes.

(!) The word must be split across two or more words. A word hidden inside another word does not count.

TIP There are only three possible letter combinations between every two **adjacent** words.

Answer: I wonder how she did in her maths test.   _____ **shed** _____

Find the hidden four-letter word in each sentence below. Underline the word and write it on the line.

1.   Have you seen them eat their meal yet?   _____

2.   My uncle had his own aeroplane.   _____

3.   You need a warm oven for baking bread.   _____

4.   The dreadful storm was a weather disaster.   _____

5.   I want to jog one mile each day.   _____

6.   Nervously, the competitors entered the ring.   _____

7.   Kimberly scored the most points in the test.   _____

8.   He was the first opponent to cross the line.   _____

9.   There was a sudden thunder crash.   _____

10.   New employees bring new ideas.   _____

(!) The hidden word may span three words. For example: She was a medal winner at the Olympics. (**same**)

Schofield & Sims

Join two words to make one

In these questions, you are given two groups of words. You have to find the two words (one from each group) that together make one new word.

Underline the **two** words, **one** from each group, that together make **one** new word. The word from the first group comes first.

(day night moon)   (sleep over mare)

Try each word in the first group with each word in the second until you find a word.

day + sleep = **daysleep**   Is this a real word?   No.

day + over = **dayover**   Is this a real word?   No.

day + mare = **daymare**   Is this a real word?   No.

night + sleep = **nightsleep**   Is this a real word?   No.

night + over = **nightover**   Is this a real word?   No.

night + mare = **nightmare**   Is this a real word?   Yes.

 The word may sound correct but make sure that it is spelt correctly too.

Write the word down. Does it look correct?

Answer: nightmare

 Underline the **two** words, **one** from each group, that together make **one** new word. The word from the first group comes first.

1.   (can key car)   (band board bored)

2.   (puff poor peer)   (on in out)

3.   (by but be)   (hind hound hand)

4.   (end and under)   (less loss lass)

5.   (about over even)   (near give take)

6.   (paint path pass)   (port part pant)

7.   (leg foot arm)   (your our their)

8.   (try in rest)   (quest round down)

9.   (see look hear)   (twenty five ten)

10.   (sign train grow)   (ape post aim)

TIP If you cannot find the new word, write down all the possible combinations. The correct one is then easier to spot.

The sound of two words may change when they are put together.

car + rot = **carrot**   The long **ar** sound in **car** changes to a short **a** sound when put together with **rot**.

prim + ate = **primate**   The short **i** sound changes to a long sound when the words are combined.

tea + ring = **tearing**   The long **ee** sound in **tea** changes to an **air** sound when joined with **ring**.

As you read the words, experiment with the letter sounds.

Change the vowel sound from long to short or short to long.

Think about the letter blends (for example, **th**, **oo**, **ea**). If one word ends in **t** and another begins with **h** there is a **th** sound in the middle of the new word. For example, **slit** + **her** = **slither**. The **t** and **h** combine to make **th**.

 Underline the **two** words, **one** from each group, that together make **one** new word. The word from the first group comes first.

11. (tar bar car)   (grin gain ten)

12. (post most pine)   (age and or)

13. (is us as)   (queen king prince)

14. (yes not all)   (is in ice)

15. (up so it)   (lid led lad)

16. (he him her)   (row air art)

17. (miss to let)   (wards take end)

18. (blue pink red)   (ant one win)

19. (tear bar out)   (round key row)

20. (and out so)   (at on off)

> **TIP** Look out for common word endings in the second group, such as **–ing**, **–er**, **–en**, **–le**, **–y**. Think about how they sound at the end of a word.

Join two words to make one

You may be asked to find one word that can go in front of a group of words to make a new set of words. You may also be asked to find a word that goes after a group of words to make a new set of words. A word that goes in front is called a prefix and a word that goes after is called a suffix.

Find **one** word that can be put in front of each of these words to make four new words.

coat   bow   storm   proof

Think of as many words as you can that end with the first word (in this example, words ending with **coat** include **overcoat**, **turncoat**, **raincoat**).

Try out each prefix (in this example, **over**, **turn**, **rain**) with the other words given, working from left to right.

over + coat = **overcoat**   Is this a real word?   Yes.

over + bow = **overbow**   Is this a real word?   No.

turn + coat = **turncoat**   Is this a real word?   Yes.

turn + bow = **turnbow**   Is this a real word?   No.

rain + coat = **raincoat**   Is this a real word?   Yes.

rain + bow = **rainbow**   Is this a real word?   Yes.

rain + storm = **rainstorm**   Is this a real word?   Yes.

rain + proof = **rainproof**   Is this a real word?   Yes.

Answer: rain

Find **one** word that can be put in front of each of these words to make four new words.

21.	time	light	dream	break	_____
22.	fall	front	bed	wheel	_____
23.	shell	shore	weed	sick	_____
24.	set	shine	down	tan	_____
25.	pack	wards	hand	ground	_____

Find **one** word that can be added to the end of each of the following words to make three new correctly spelt words.

26. sub _____   hall _____   mid _____

27. work _____   fall _____   with _____

28. eaves _____   dew _____   tear _____

29. blue _____   foot _____   finger _____

30. fire _____   down _____   lake _____

Add or remove a letter to make a new word

This question type tests your spelling skills by asking you to add or remove letters from a given word in order to make a new word.

You may be asked to add the same letter to the beginning of a number of given words so that they all make new words.

> Which **one** letter can be added to the beginning of each of the words below to make new words?
>
> ___ ale   ___ lime   ___ parks   ___ cold

Try each letter of the alphabet at the start of the first word. Make a note of the letters that can be added to **ale** to make a new word.

bale, dale, gale, hale, kale, male, pale, sale, tale, vale

Next try each of these letters at the beginning of the second word and make a note of the letters that can be added to **lime** to make a new word. Only **s** creates a new word – **slime**.

Now check that adding **s** to the beginning of each of the remaining words creates two new words.

sparks and **scold** are both words, so **s** is the answer.

Answer: s

Which **one** letter can be added to the beginning of each of the words below to make new words?

1. ___ rifts   ___ rake   ___ elude   ___ amp

2. ___ ours   ___ airy   ___ over   ___ ill

3. ___ roll   ___ weak   ___ witch   ___ able

4. ___ live   ___ men   ___ zone   ___ pens

5. ___ gain   ___ part   ___ top   ___ wry

6. ___ lock   ___ ream   ___ lamp   ___ old

7. ___ light   ___ rook   ___ eat   ___ end

8. ___ hoot   ___ tale   ___ hock   ___ liver

> **TIP** If you are given multiple-choice answer options, you only need to try the letters given as options.

Add or remove a letter to make a new word

You may be asked to add or remove a letter from anywhere in a word to change its meaning.

Remove **one** letter from the word in capitals to make a new word. The meaning of the new word is given in brackets. Write the word on the line.

AMBLE (to have the skill to do something) _____

Work through the word to see which letters can be removed to make a new word.

Remove **A**: mble   mble is not a word.

Remove **M**: able   able is a word.

When you find a letter that can be removed to leave a new word, check that the new word has the same meaning as given in the brackets. **Able** means 'to have the skill to do something', so this is the correct answer.

Answer: ABLE

> **TIP** Sometimes, two or more different letters can be removed to leave a new word. You must check which word has the meaning given in the brackets.

You might also be asked to add a letter to a word in capitals to make a new word. Look carefully at the word and meaning you are given and use both of these clues to help you identify the new word. Look out for examples of this question type in the practice questions.

Remove **one** letter from the word in capitals to make a new word. The meaning of the new word is given in brackets. Write the word on the line.

9.   **SEWED** (a pip or grain)   _____

10.   **FIENDS** (resists an attack)   _____

11.   **CREAM** (to fill something until it is almost overflowing)   _____

12.   **GRANT** (to complain loudly about something at length)   _____

Add **one** letter to the word in capitals to make a new word. The meaning of the new word is given in brackets. Write the word on the line.

13.   **BUSES** (shrubs or hedges)   _____

14.   **DOZE** (a group of twelve)   _____

15.   **ITCH** (a trench or channel)   _____

16.   **LOSE** (a small insect that lives on mammals or birds)   _____

Spot spelling mistakes

This type of question tests your spelling skills. You may be asked to spot a word that has been spelt incorrectly, to choose the correct spelling of a word to complete a sentence, or to add letters to a word so that it is spelt correctly.

The sentence below contains a word that is spelt incorrectly. Underline the word and write its correct spelling on the line.

I wrote the adress on the envelope. _____

Look out for words that are spelt using double letters, silent letters and unstressed vowels (where a vowel is not sounded in the way that you would expect, like the first **a** in **separate**). To help you remember the correct spelling, emphasise it as you read the word. For example, you could read **separate** as **sep-ar-ate** until you find that you can easily remember the unstressed **a**.

Answer: I wrote the <u>adress</u> on the envelope. _____**address**_____

Complete the sentence below by filling in the missing letters.

The f __ __ r c e dog guarded the entrance to the tunnel.

Read the sentence and see if your brain completes the word as you read. If it does not, use the context of the sentence to help you. Think about an adjective beginning with **f** that could describe a guard dog.

Once you have identified the word, think about how it should be spelt. If you are not sure, try writing down different ways that the word might be spelt and see which one looks correct.

The answer to this question is **fierce**.

Answer: The f _i_ _e_ r c e dog guarded the entrance to the tunnel.

(TIP) The rhyme **i** before **e**, except after **c**, and only when the word rhymes with **see** helps you remember which way round the **i** and **e** should be. However, there are some exceptions to this rule, which you must also learn.

Each sentence below contains a word that is spelt incorrectly. Underline the word and write its correct spelling on the line.

1.   I want to enroll in the flower arranging class.   _____

2.   The suprise birthday party was a memorable occasion.   _____

Underline the correct spelling of the word that completes the sentence.

3.   The actor did not audition for the musical / musicull / musicle because he could not sing.

4.   Open your him / hym / hymn book to the first page.

Complete each sentence below by filling in the missing letters.

5.   Hugo paid the bill and then checked his r e c __ __ p t.

6.   The cave s h __ __ l d e d the travellers from the storm.

Anagrams

This question type tests your vocabulary and spelling skills. You will be given a word which has had its letters jumbled up. You must unjumble the letters to find the word. To help you, the word might be included in a sentence or you may be given a clue about the word's meaning.

Unjumble the letters of the word in capitals. The word should complete the sentence so that it makes sense. Write your answer on the line.

The SNTLPA in the garden had wilted. _____

Read the sentence. You may find that your brain naturally unjumbles the word as you read.

If the answer does not come to you straight away, use the context of the sentence to help you work out what the word might be. The jumbled word is something that can be found in a garden and that can wilt.

FLOWERS are found in the garden and can wilt, but the letters **SNTLPA** cannot be rearranged to spell this word.

PLANTS are found in the garden and can wilt. The letters **SNTLPA** can be rearranged to spell this word.

Check if your answer makes sense in the sentence: The plants in the garden had wilted.

Answer: The SNTLPA in the garden had wilted. _____**PLANTS**_____

> (!) You may be given a sentence that contains **two** jumbled words. You should follow the same steps as above, using clues from the sentence to help you work out what the words should be. Look out for questions of this type in the practice questions.

Unjumble the letters of the word in capitals. The word should complete the sentence so that it makes sense. Write your answer on the line.

1. She did not know how to NSOPEDR _____ to the question.

2. The sweet liquid was thick and YPYRUS _____.

3. A male KNICCHE _____ is called a EROSTOR _____.

4. The NUCEAIDE _____ cheered loudly as the RAHCORTSE

   _____ bowed.

5. I bought an old ANGITPNI _____ from the EQINATU

   _____ dealer.

6. My RHCIO _____ is performing at the EHTATER

   _____ on Saturday.

Sometimes, the jumbled word will not be contained in a sentence. Instead, you may be given a clue as to its meaning. The clue might give the definition of the word, or you might be given two other words that are linked to the word you are trying to find.

Unjumble the letters in capitals to make a word. The word is linked to the first two words. Write your answer on the line.

horn   deer   REALNT   _____

Look at the clues.

A **horn** could be something that makes a blaring sound, or it could be a bony outgrowth on an animal. Since the next clue is **deer**, it seems more likely that the clue refers to an animal horn.

Look at the letters and see if you can rearrange them to make a word that is linked to **horn** and **deer**.

Answer: horn   deer   REALNT   _____**ANTLER**_____

TIP If you struggle to rearrange the letters in your head, you can try writing them in a circle. Doing this can make it easier to spot the word. Remember that the word you make must be linked to the two clue words. If you rearrange the letters into a word but it does not link to the clue words, this will not be the answer.

Unjumble the letters in capitals to make a word. Use the clue on the left to help you. Write your answer on the line.

7.   uncover   ERVLEA   _____

8.   barter   NBAGIAR   _____

9.   thrive   SLUOFHRI   _____

Unjumble the letters in capitals to make a word. The word is linked to the first two words. Write your answer on the line.

10.   insect   sport   IEKTRCC   _____

11.   balance   fish   EHRPC   _____

12.   injury   wrapped   DONWU   _____

Find the letter missing from the muddled word

This question type tests your spelling skills, vocabulary and ability to identify the context of a sentence. You are given a sentence in which two of the words have had their letters muddled up. The muddled words have both had the same letter removed. You must work out what the words should be and identify the letter that is missing from both words.

The sentence below contains two words that have had their letters muddled up. Both words have had the same letter removed from them. Put the letters in order and find the letter that is missing from both. Write your answer on the line.

The **HCIT** cackled as she **DEAV** her wand. _____

First, read the sentence to get a sense of its context. It is about a woman with a wand. Think of some words that could describe such a person – 'magician', 'warlock', 'witch'. Compare the words you have thought of to the muddled letters in the sentence. **Witch** has the letters **HCIT**, meaning the missing letter could be **W**.

Now look at the second muddled word. Using **W** along with the letters, could you make a word that fits the sentence? Think about the position of the muddled word in the sentence to help you. It will be a verb, so it is likely that the word will end in **ED**.

___ ___ ___ E D   **A**, **V** and **W** must go in front of the **ED** in an order that makes a word.

___ A ___ E D   Think about spelling rules. **A** must be in this position because there are no words where **V** and **W** are next to one another.

W A V E D   The muddled word could be **WAVED**.

Check that the two words make sense in the sentence: The **WITCH** cackled as she **WAVED** her wand. They do, so the answer is **W**.

Answer: The **HCIT** cackled as she **DEAV** her wand.   **W**

TIP Most words contain at least one vowel. If the muddled word only contains consonants, the missing letter is likely to be a vowel, although you should watch out for words that use **y** instead.

The sentences below contain two words that have had their letters muddled up. Both words have had the same letter removed from them. Put the letters in order and find the letter that is missing from both. Write your answer on the line.

1. I put the lollipop **KCST** into the black **BSHBUR** bag. _____

2. The van's **RKBES** were so **YQEUSK** that they sounded like mice. _____

3. We bought our pet **BIRBA** a new **UCHH**. _____

4. The **YKUET** squawked excitedly as it pecked at the **INAG**. _____

5. We had **HTOTHU** that we would see a **RAFEFI** at the zoo. _____

6. He is going to the **ERATHT** this **IVNENG** to see a play. _____

This question type requires you to write words into a grid. So that all the words can fit, they will overlap one another by sharing letters. You must work out which words should be placed where in order for them all to fit.

There are two types of word grid. The first type looks like a crossword puzzle. You will be given a starting letter to help.

Fit these words into the blank spaces in the word grid. Use all of the words. One letter has been placed into the grid to help you.

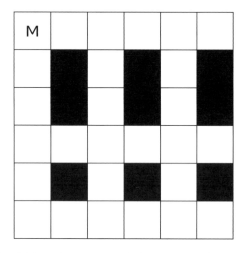

merges

gulped

strays

taller

mettle

lonely

Look at the positon of the letter you have been given. The **M** will be the first letter of two different words in the grid. Look at the word list and find any words that begin with **M**.

Merges and **mettle** begin with **M**. Think carefully about which word will be placed where. If **merges** is written down the left-hand side of the grid, **S** will be the first letter of the word across the bottom. If **mettle** is written down the left-hand side of the grid, **E** will be the first letter of the word across the bottom.

Look at the word list again – are there any words that start with **S** or **E**? **Strays** begins with **S** but there are no words that begin with **E**. This means it must be **merges** that should be written down the left-hand side. **Mettle** must be written along the top. **Strays** can then be fitted into the blanks along the bottom.

Use the letters you have filled in to work out how to fit the remaining words into the grid.

M	E	T	T	L	E
E	■		■		■
R	■		■		■
G					
E	■		■		■
S	T	R	A	Y	S

Answer:

M	E	T	T	L	E
E	■	A	■	O	■
R	■	L	■	N	■
G	U	L	P	E	D
E	■	E	■	L	■
S	T	R	A	Y	S

Word grids

The second type of word grid you might come across is a blank square with space for nine letters.

Fit these words into the blank grid so that you can read all the words, either from left to right or from top to bottom.
Use all of the words.

tea   par   asp   ate   ear   sea

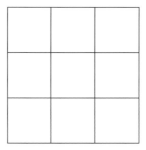

Consider the middle square in the grid. Two words will share this letter as their middle letter when they are fitted into the grid. Look at the list of words and see which words have the same middle letter.

There are different pairs of words that share the same middle letter: **tea** and **sea**, and **par** and **ear**. These pairs of words can be written across the middle of the grid, like this:

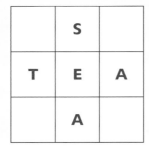   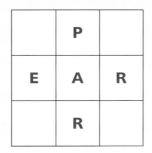

 TIP   Since the grid is a square, it does not matter whether **tea** and **sea**, and **par** and **ear** are written left to right or top to bottom, as long as they cross over one another in the middle.

You must now work out which of these pairs can stay in position and fit the other words in the grid around it. Look at the last letters of each word. They will be the middle letters of the words written along the bottom and the right-hand side of the grid. Look at the word list and see if there are any words with **A** or **R** as their middle letter.

There are two words with **A** as their middle letter and none with **R**, so it must be **tea** and **sea** that cross over in the middle of the grid.

To place the remaining words into the grid, look at their middle letters. **Asp** has an **S** in the middle, so it must be written along the top of the grid. Once you have fitted the third word into the grid, you should find it straightforward to fill in the rest.

Answer:

A	S	P
T	E	A
E	A	R

Now answer the following questions.

1. Fit these words into the blank spaces in the word grid. Use all of the words. One letter has been placed into the grid to help you.

really   higher   oxtail

herald   deadly   haloed

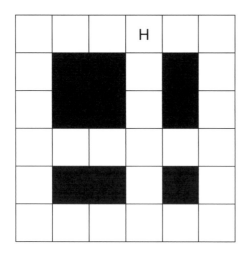

3. Fit these words into the blank grid so that you can read all the words, either from left to right or from top to bottom. Use all of the words.

ice   tar   spa

era   cap   its

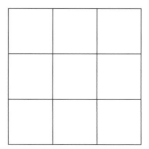

2. Fit these words into the blank spaces in the word grid. Use all of the words. One letter has been placed into the grid to help you.

dreams   tokens   bought

attack   beamed   uptake

4. Fit these words into the blank grid so that you can read all the words, either from left to right or from top to bottom. Use all of the words.

two   web   orb

ebb   the   her

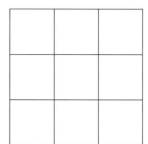

Now test your skills with these practice pages. If you get stuck, go back to pages 63 to 84 for some reminders.

Missing letter

Find the **one** missing letter that will complete both pairs of words. It will end the words before the brackets and start the words after the brackets.

1. arm (____) our   pla (____) acht

2. clo (____) oal   han (____) ive

3. mat (____) asy   win (____) ven

Find **two** letters that will end the first word and begin the second word.

4. ear (____ ____) read

5. san (____ ____) namic

6. gold (____ ____) ough

Move a letter

Move **one** letter from the first word to the second word to make **two** new words. Write the new words on the lines.

7. wheat   wed   _____ _____

8. shave   barn   _____ _____

9. cream   trip   _____ _____

10. naive   led   _____ _____

11. pleat   mode   _____ _____

12. could   bond   _____ _____

Word ladders

Change the first word into the last word. Change only one letter at a time and make a new, different word in the middle.

13. TRIED   _____ FREED

14. MOUNT   _____ SOUND

15. BLINK   _____ CLICK

Change the first word into the last word. Change only one letter at a time and make **two** new, different words in the middle.

16. STARS   _____ _____ SCANT

17. WATER   _____ _____ SAFES

18. TRAIN   _____ _____ BRAND

Spelling practice page 2

Missing three letters

The word in capitals has had three letters next to each other taken out. These three letters make one correctly spelt word without changing the order. Write the word on the line.

1. Can you **AGE** to eat any more? _____

2. The playground had a swing and a **SE**. _____

3. I had to write a long **ES** for my coursework. _____

4. The **SNING** top whirled round and round. _____

Words with letters in common

Underline the only word that **can** be made using the letters of the word on the left.

5. ANOTHER   antler   there   neither   throne   hereto

Underline the only word that **cannot** be made using the letters of the word on the left.

6. DEHYDRATE   heard   dryer   tree   rated   heady

In each group of words below, circle the **two** words that are spelt using the same letters.

7. THIRD THIGH GIRTH RIGHT TIGHT   8. SHALE LEASE SALES LEASH SLASH

Spot the word

Find the hidden four-letter word in each sentence below. Underline the word and write it on the line.

9. She smiled her brightest smile. _____

10. Laugh and smile every day! _____

11. He arrived late and Mum was cross. _____

12. It's important not to waste a minute! _____

Join two words to make one

Underline the **two** words, **one** from each group, that together make **one** new word. The word from the first group comes first.

13. (up count sing)   (out down in)   14. (round under through)   (above below about)

Find **one** word that can be put in front of each of these words to make four new words.

15. doors   live   pouring   station   _____

16. king   sure   certain   cent   _____

Schofield & Sims

Add or remove a letter to make a new word

Which **one** letter can be added to the beginning of each of the words below to make new words?

1. ___ hip   ___ over   ___ lose   ___ are

Remove **one** letter from the word in capitals to make a new word. The meaning of the new word is given in brackets. Write the word on the line.

2. **PRINT**   (a measure of capacity) _____

Add **one** letter to the word in capitals to make a new word. The meaning of the new word is given in brackets. Write the word on the line.

3. **BRIDE**   (a crossing from one side of an obstacle to another) _____

Spot spelling mistakes

The sentence below contains a word that is spelt incorrectly. Underline the word and write its correct spelling on the line.

4. If you fasten the knot too losely it might come undone. _____

Underline the correct spelling of the word that completes the sentence.

5. She could not spot the diffrence / difference / difrence between the two images.

Complete the sentence below by filling in the missing letters.

6. The naughty puppy enjoyed causing m i s c h ___ ___ f.

Anagrams

Unjumble the letters of the word in capitals. The word should complete the sentence so that it makes sense. Write your answer on the line.

7. Kieran decided to avoid an NTMEAGUR _____ and gave his sister the television remote.

8. I always ECEBRATEL _____ my birthday at my favourite TANRESUTRA

    _____ .

Unjumble the letters in capitals to make a word. Use the clue on the left to help you. Write your answer on the line.

9. triple EBLERT _____   10. croaky AHOSER _____

Unjumble the letters in capitals to make a word. The word is linked to the first two words. Write your answer on the line.

11. glide   seashore   ASOCT _____

Find the letter missing from the muddled word

The sentences below contain two words that have had their letters muddled up. Both words have had the same letter removed from them. Put the letters in order and find the letter that is missing from both. Write your answer on the line.

1. **ERSPU** was a slice of birthday cake left over from the **AYRT**. ____

2. Alexa **ATSEE** her brother until her mother **UTSEHO** at her to stop. ____

3. The elderly woman **EKPS** so **FTYSL** that it was difficult to hear what she was saying. ____

Word grids

4. Fit these words into the blank spaces in the word grid. Use all of the words. One letter has been placed into the grid to help you.

   aphids   enzyme   aflame

   chaste   fourth   fruity

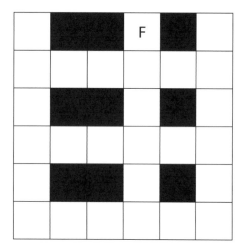

5. Fit these words into the blank grid so that you can read all the words, either from left to right or from top to bottom. Use all of the words.

   rue   age   ink

   eke   gnu   air

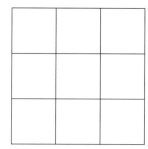

Schofield & Sims

Select words to complete a sentence

This question type tests your ability to interpret the context of a sentence and identify words that make sense within this context.

You may be asked to select the word or words that best complete a sentence or identify a word that does not fit a sentence and exchange it for one that does.

You may also be asked to complete a statement with a word that makes the statement true.

> From each set of brackets, select the word that completes the sentence in the best way. Underline your answers.
>
> I opened the (door, carpet, book), turned to the (none, first, middle) page and began the
>
> (story, end, tail).

Read the whole sentence to get a sense of its context.

You can then split the sentence into sections and think about which word makes sense in each of them. However, you must also consider which words best fit the context of the whole sentence.

Section 1: 'I opened the (door, ~~carpet~~, <u>book</u>)'

I cannot open a carpet so this cannot be the answer. Lightly cross it out. I can open a door or a book, so either of these would make sense. However, the sentence tells me that the item I open must have pages. A door does not have pages but a book does, so 'book' fits the sentence.

Section 2: 'turned to the (~~none~~, <u>first</u>, middle) page'

'None' page does not make sense, so lightly cross out 'none'. I can turn to the first or the middle page of a book, so either of these words would make sense. However, the sentence uses the word 'began', which tells me that I must be at the beginning of something, so 'first' fits the sentence better than 'middle'.

Section 3: 'and began the (<u>story</u>, end, ~~tail~~)'

Be careful not to be caught out by homophones! 'Tale' would fit the sentence, but 'tail' does not. It makes more sense to begin a story than to begin an end, so 'story' fits this section better than 'end'.

Once you think you have selected the correct words, check that the sentence makes sense.

Answer: I opened the (door, carpet, <u>book</u>), turned to the (none, <u>first</u>, middle) page and began the (<u>story</u>, end, tail).

Sometimes, the answer options are not set out in brackets but are listed below the sentence. Follow the same method, but check the instructions carefully for how you should mark your answer.

Select words to complete a sentence

Here, you are asked to replace a word to make a sentence make sense.

For the sentence below to make sense, one word needs to be taken out and a different word added in its place. Underline the word that should be taken out and write the word that should be added in its place on the line.

The bird tapped its beak on the window and roared. _____

Read the sentence and think about why it does not make sense. Birds do not roar, so either 'bird' or 'roared' does not make sense in the sentence. If 'bird' was swapped for an animal that does roar, for example a lion, would the sentence make sense?

The LION tapped its beak on the window and roared.

The sentence still does not make sense – a lion does not have a beak!

If 'roared' was swapped for a noise that a bird could make, would the sentence make sense?

The bird tapped its beak on the window and CHIRPED.

Yes, now the sentence makes sense.

Underline 'roared' and write 'chirped' (or another sound that a bird could make) on the line.

Answer: The bird tapped its beak on the window and <u>roared</u>. _____**chirped**_____

 TIP If you are changing a verb, remember to write your new word in the correct tense for the sentence.

In this example, you need to pick a word to make the statement true.

Choose the word or phrase that makes the statement true. Underline your answer.

All plants need (soil, a pot, leaves, water, a garden) to grow.

All of these words make sense in the context of the sentence. However, you need to find the word that makes the statement true. Ask yourself which word makes the sentence true:

Do all plants need <u>soil</u> to grow? No – cacti grow in deserts.

Do all plants need <u>a pot</u> to grow? No – plants grow in the wild.

Do all plants need <u>leaves</u> to grow? No – mushrooms don't have leaves.

Do all plants need <u>water</u> to grow? Yes – all plants need water.

Do all plants need <u>a garden</u> to grow? No – plants grow in the wild.

Only one word makes the statement true – all plants need <u>water</u> to grow.

Answer: All plants need (soil, a pot, leaves, <u>water</u>, a garden) to grow.

Select words to complete a sentence

From each set of brackets, select the word that completes each sentence below in the best way. Underline your answers.

1. The (boy, horses, children) laughed as they (teased, threw, play) each other on their way (underground, home, tomorrow).

2. Recorders are my favourite type of (instrument, technology, utensil) because they make a (harsher, enjoyment, gentle) sound which I (appreciative, adore, loathe).

Select the word that completes each sentence below in the best way. Circle your answer. Then write it on the line.

3. The restaurant received _____ complaints about its inhospitable staff.

   A. abnormal   **B.** treacherous   **C.** numerous   **D.** frequently   **E.** ignored

4. She proceeded _____ as she was frightened of losing her way.

   A. confidently   **B.** careful   **C.** warning   **D.** scarcely   **E.** cautiously

For each sentence below to make sense, one word needs to be taken out and a different word added in its place. Underline the word that should be taken out and write the word that should be added in its place on the line.

5. It was so dark in the pitch-black cave that Lilian could barely taste anything.   _____

6. I saw my favourite song playing on the radio.   _____

7. The grateful king punished the brave knight for his courage.   _____

Choose the word or phrase that makes each statement below true. Underline your answer.

8. Fictional stories are always (long, exciting, imaginary, enjoyable, interesting).

9. Bungalows are never built with (stairs, windows, a door, a roof, a conservatory).

10. All doctors are highly (friendly, exhausting, judgemental, sympathetic, trained).

Homophones

Homophones are words that sound the same but have different meanings and, usually, different spellings. You may be asked to identify the correct homophone to complete a sentence, or to find homophones that have been used incorrectly.

Underline the words that complete the sentence in the best way.

The *weather / whether has bean / been* stormy this month.

Think carefully about the context in which the words are being used. The sentence is describing what the weather has been like recently, so it is these words that you must underline.

Answer: The <u>*weather*</u> / *whether has bean* / <u>*been*</u> stormy this month.

 Underline the words that complete each sentence in the best way.

1. My friends left to *by / buy / bye* sweets even though I had asked them to *wait / weight* for me.

2. The hikers could not see the *root / route* on *their / they're / there* map.

3. Lana must *wrap / rap* the presents before she is *aloud / allowed* to watch television.

In the sentence below, underline the **two** homophones that have been used incorrectly.

The boy chose to lye to his mother about how his genes had become muddy.

Read the sentence carefully and see whether any of the words stand out as being spelt incorrectly. The verb **lie** is spelt with an **i** so **lye** is being used incorrectly here. Underline **lye**.

If words do not seem to stand out, think about which words could be homophones. Make a note of these words and the different spellings and meanings they can have.

boy – a male child   **buoy** – a float   **genes** – DNA   **jeans** – denim trousers

Use the context of the sentence to help you decide which word is needed. A **boy** might lie to his mother and **jeans** might become muddy. Underline **genes**.

Answer: The boy chose to <u>lye</u> to his mother about how his <u>genes</u> had become muddy.

 In each of the passages below, underline the **five** homophones that have been used incorrectly.

4. Grandmother was making doe in the kitchen. I watched as she needed it carefully, wrinkling her nose as flour billowed up from the table. The cent of baking filled the air and I side happily. I had mist her terribly while she had been gone.

5. The kernel examined the soldiers closely. She was known four punishing troupes for miner mistakes. However, she had earned their trussed as a strong leader.

6. As his father's sole air, Jacob inherited the entire fortune. He was especially pleased to receive a beautiful peace of jewellery. It was a silver broach decorated with pail gemstones and purls.

Select words to complete a paragraph

This type of question requires you to choose the correct words to complete a paragraph. It tests your ability to identify sentence context and word definitions.

Using each of the words in the box below once, complete the paragraph by filling in the missing words.

perplex	herds	recognise	temperature
individuals	common	species	purpose

Three different _____ of zebra inhabit Africa. The most

_____ is called the plains zebra, which is found in the south and

east of the continent. Zebras are well known for their stripy coats but zoologists are

not entirely sure what _____ these stripes serve. It could be that

they _____ predators or they may help the zebra to control its

body _____. Since every zebra has a unique pattern of stripes,

they may also help zebras to _____ one another. Zebras live in

_____. When the animals migrate, the herds travel together in groups

which can reach as many as 1000 _____.

Read the words in the box and think about what each of them means. Do not panic if there are some words that you do not recognise – it may be that you can still answer the question.

Next read the paragraph, ignoring the gaps in the text. Once you understand what the text is about, re-read the text and fill in any gaps that you know. As you fill in each gap, lightly cross out the word you have used from the box above. If you are not sure which word goes in a gap, leave that one out.

Once you have filled in all the gaps you know, look at the words and gaps you have remaining. Think about which of the remaining words would make sense in the gap. You can use clues in the paragraph to help you. Should the word be an adjective, noun, adverb or verb? Should the word be a plural? Should it start with a vowel or a consonant? If you are still not sure, try each remaining word in the gap and choose the one that makes the most sense.

When you have filled in the gaps, read the whole paragraph again and check it makes sense.

Answer: Three different _____**species**_____ of zebra inhabit Africa. The most

_____**common**_____ is called the plains zebra, which is found in the south and east of the

continent. Zebras are well known for their stripy coats but zoologists are not entirely sure what

_____**purpose**_____ these stripes serve. It could be that they _____**perplex**_____

predators or they may help the zebra to control its body _____**temperature**_____. Since every

zebra has a unique pattern of stripes, they may also help zebras to _____**recognise**_____

one another. Zebras live in _____**herds**_____. When the animals migrate, the herds travel

together in groups which can reach as many as 1000 _____**individuals**_____.

Select words to complete a paragraph

✎ Now answer the following questions.

1. Using each of the words in the box below once, complete the paragraph by filling in the missing words.

expanded	population	centre	territories
architecture	reigned	unhygienic	advanced

At its most powerful, the Roman Empire _____ over more than 45 million

people and encompassed _____ across Europe, North Africa and Asia.

As the empire _____ , so too did its _____ , Rome,

which grew from a town to a large, bustling city. Rome was home to over one million

subjects. Although it is now celebrated for its beautiful _____ and

_____ technology, its vast _____ meant that the city

was also a hazardous, _____ place to live.

2. Using each of the words in the box below once, complete the paragraph by filling in the missing words.

jeers	ordered	daring	occasionally
snatched	antelope	declined	sobbing

The new boy went off brushing the dust from his clothes, _____ ,

snuffling, and _____ looking back and shaking his head and threatening

what he would do to Tom the "next time he caught him out." To which Tom responded with

_____ , and started off in high feather, and as soon as his back was turned

the new boy _____ up a stone, threw it and hit him between the

shoulders and then turned tail and ran like an _____. Tom chased the

traitor home, and thus found out where he lived. He then held a position at the gate for some

time, _____ the enemy to come outside, but the enemy only made faces

at him through the window and _____. At last the enemy's mother

appeared, and called Tom a bad, vicious, vulgar child, and _____ him away.

From *The Adventures of Tom Sawyer* by Mark Twain

Schofield & Sims

Rearrange words to make a sentence

This question type tests your understanding of sentence construction. You will be given a sentence that does not make sense. You must swap the position of two of the words in the sentence so that it does make sense.

Underline the two words that need to swap places in the sentence below for it to make sense.

The shelves kept many novels on its bookshop.

When you read the sentence you may find it easy to spot which two words need to switch position.

If the answer does not come to you straight away, think about why the sentence does not make sense. It is not usual to describe shelves as 'keeping' something.

The **shelves kept** many novels **on its bookshop**.

Items are usually found **in** a bookshop, rather than **on** one.

Now consider which words in these two sections of the sentence could be swapped so that the sentence makes sense. A bookshop could keep items and items could be kept on a shelf. If **shelves** and **bookshop** switched places, the sentence would make sense: 'The bookshop kept many novels on its shelves'.

Underline **shelves** and **bookshop** to show that these two words should swap position.

Answer: The <u>shelves</u> kept many novels on its <u>bookshop</u>.

 In each sentence below, underline the two words that need to swap places for it to make sense.

1. The farmer dozen a counted eggs.

2. The land is difficult without navigate to a map.

3. Green trees' leaves turned from the to yellow.

4. She every in her diary wrote day.

5. Organising the festival weeks several took.

6. The beautiful water glided through the murky swan.

7. There during a short interval was the performance.

8. He grimaced stable he cleaned out the as.

9. The was display firework spectacular.

10. His regretted he decision immediately.

Find the superfluous word

In this question type, you are given a sentence that has been jumbled up. An extra word that the sentence does not need has been added to the jumbled words. You must unjumble the words to make a sentence and find the word that is not needed. 'Superfluous' means 'not needed'.

Make a sentence using all but one of the words below. Write the sentence on the line and underline the word that you do not use.

tin its spoon and bowl I the opened contents a into poured

_____

Read the words and begin to think about how they might fit together in a sentence. You may find that you naturally begin to order the words in a way that makes sense.

If the answer does not come to you straight away, consider which words would make sense next to each other.

Think about whether the words are nouns, adjectives, verbs or adverbs and how these different types of words should be placed together. For example, an adjective will come before a noun in a sentence.

Begin to combine the words into small phrases. Keep track of the words you have used by lightly crossing them out.

~~tin~~ its spoon and ~~bowl I the opened~~ contents ~~a into poured~~

'poured into a bowl'   'I opened the tin'

Try to place these phrases together in a sentence. You may need to use connectives to fit phrases together. Look for places where any of the remaining words can be added into the sentence.

~~tin its~~ spoon and ~~bowl I the opened contents a into poured~~

Answer: tin its <u>spoon</u> and bowl I the opened contents a into poured

   I opened the tin and poured its contents into a bowl.

_____

 For each question below, make a sentence using all but one of the words. Write the sentence on the line and underline the word that you do not use.

1.   impress poor the pupil's not behaviour detention did teacher the

_____

2.   to difficult it environment silence a make noisy can concentrate

_____

3.   audience as cinema deafeningly bowed the the applauded actor

_____

4.   it harbour ship fortunately moored the in was the still

_____

Complete the word

This question type tests your vocabulary and spelling skills. You are given an extract in which there are some incomplete words. You must identify the words and add the missing letters to complete them, ensuring they are spelt correctly.

Add the missing letters to complete the words in the extract below.

The a __ t __ marched swiftly across the __ i __ n __ c blanket in a __ __ a t

line. Each time an insect discovered a forgotten plate of food it a l e __ __ __ d its

comrades with a waggle of its __ n t __ n n a __ . The procession would then move

urgently __ o __ a __ d s the newest target, e __ __ __ r to share in the bounty.

Before you try to fill in any letters, read the whole extract. Let your eyes skim over the incomplete words as you read. You may find that you naturally recognise what the word should be. If so, fill in the missing letters, taking care to spell the word correctly.

If you do not recognise the words straight away, you can use these techniques to help you to work out the answers:

- Use clues from the extract. The extract tells us that the creature marching across the blanket is an insect. Think of types of insect that begin with the letter **a** and then check whether any of the words you think of fit the gap.

- Use word connections. To work out what the insect in the extract above could be waggling, think about words that are connected with insects and their body parts. Check whether the words you think of would fit into the gap.

- Use spelling rules. In the extract, one of the incomplete words comes after the word **a** – 'a __ __ a t line'. The first letter of this word must therefore be a consonant, rather than a vowel. This technique can be helpful but it may not narrow down the possible answers sufficiently, so it is best to try the other techniques first.

Read back over the extract as you complete words to make sure they make sense and to help shed new light on what the remaining words could be.

Answer:

The a **n** t **s** marched swiftly across the **p** i **c** n **i** c blanket in a **n** **e** a t

line. Each time an insect discovered a forgotten plate of food it a l e **r** **t** **e** d its

comrades with a waggle of its **a** n t **e** n n a **e** . The procession would then move

urgently **t** o **w** a **r** d s the newest target, e **a** **g** e r to share in the bounty.

Complete the word

You may see this question type presented in a different way. You may be given an extract with incomplete words but, instead of filling in the letters, you may be asked to write the complete word beside the extract like this:

The a __ t __ marched swiftly across the
__ i __ n __ c blanket in a __ __ a t line.
Each time an insect discovered a forgotten plate
of food it a l e __ __ __ d its comrades
with a waggle of its __ n t __ n n a __.

i) ants

ii) picnic

iii) neat

iv) alerted

v) antennae

Add the missing letters to complete the words in each extract below.

1. The door was locked and although he r __ t __ l __ d the handle vigorously, Romit
could not __ __ r c e it open. He k __ __ __ t down and peeked
c u __ __ __ u __ l y through the keyhole. The room on the other side of the door was
dark and it took his eyes a moment to a __ j __ __ t. Slowly, he b __ __ __ n to
make out ominous black shapes crouched in the __ h __ d __ w s.

2. As the waves crashed around the little boat, the __ a __ t __ __ n gripped the ship's
wheel so t __ __ h t __ y his k __ u c __ l __ s turned white. He desperately
wanted his c __ __ w to r __ t __ e __ t below deck but they __ e __ __ s e d
to l __ __ v e his side.

In each extract below there are **five** incomplete words. Write the complete words, correctly spelt, on the lines to the right of the box.

3.

The eagle looked m a __ __ s __ i c as it soared
__ b o __ e us. It was h __ __ __ i n g, its
sharp t __ l __ __ s ready to s __ a __ c h
unsuspecting prey.

i) _____

ii) _____

iii) _____

iv) _____

v) _____

4.

My f __ __ __ u r __ t e fruit is pomegranate.
It can be tricky to __ r e p __ __ e, however the
d e __ __ c __ o __ s taste of its j __ __ __ y,
ruby-coloured seeds is worth the e __ f __ __ t.

i) _____

ii) _____

iii) _____

iv) _____

v) _____

Schofield & Sims

Now test your skills with these practice pages. If you get stuck, go back to pages 89 to 98 for some reminders.

Select words to complete a sentence

From each set of brackets, select the word that completes each sentence below in the best way. Underline your answers.

1. Dhrooti's (ambition, fear, imagination) was to (discover, invent, become) a scientist so she

    studied (constantly, occasionally, infrequently).

2. The (music, audience, moment) fell silent as the (clumsy, tuneful, elegant) dancers sprang onto

    the (stage, balcony, programme).

Select the word that completes each sentence below in the best way. Circle your answer. Then write it on the line.

3. Gleaming gold shone from _____ the sleeping dragon's belly.

    A. above   **B.** adjacent   **C.** beneath   **D.** nearby   **E.** surrounding

4. Although he had been _____ to go to the party, he very much enjoyed it.

    A. excited   **B.** lonely   **C.** eager   **D.** reluctant   **E.** encourage

For each sentence below to make sense, one word needs to be taken out and a different word added in its place. Underline the word that should be taken out and write the word that should be added in its place on the line.

5. The tree's roots moved gently in the wind.   _____

6. The teacher punished the students for their neat work and tidy desks.   _____

Choose the word or phrase that makes each statement below true. Underline your answer.

7. Humans need (milk, oxygen, limbs, friends, comfort) to survive.

8. All swans are (white, aggressive, dangerous, female, waterfowl).

Homophones

Underline the words that complete each sentence in the best way.

9. All of the *stationery / stationary* on the desk is *blue / blew*.

10. Which way is it *two / to / too* the *peer / pier*?

11. I strolled down the *rode / road* and wandered *passed / past* the church.

In the passage below, underline the **five** homophones that have been used incorrectly.

12. The archaeologist had discovered an ancient scull. He had been discrete about his fined as

    he was sure that his employer, who did not understand how important the artefact was,

    would attempt to seas it from him and cell it.

Select words to complete a paragraph

1. Using each of the words in the box below once, complete the paragraph by filling in the missing words.

disturbances	occasional	deeply	activity
rate	dart	stages	rhythmic

Sleep occurs in cycles. Each cycle has five _____. During the first and second

stages, you sleep very lightly. Your breathing and heart _____ become

slower and _____ in your body decreases, though you may still experience

_____ muscle twitches. You begin to sleep more _____

during stages three and four. Your breathing becomes _____ and it is

difficult for you to be woken by noise or other _____. The fifth stage of

the cycle is when you dream. During this stage, your eyes _____ about

rapidly beneath your closed eyelids.

2. Using each of the words in the box below once, complete the paragraph by filling in the missing words.

sweetly	dressed	bells	gown
glistened	shade	sprinkled	brims

Three were men and one a woman, and all were oddly _____.

They wore round hats that rose to a small point a foot above their heads, with

little _____ around the _____ that tinkled

_____ as they moved. The hats of the men were blue; the little woman's

hat was white, and she wore a white _____ that hung in pleats from her

shoulders. Over it were _____ little stars that _____ in

the sun like diamonds. The men were dressed in blue, of the same _____

as their hats, and wore well-polished boots with a deep roll of blue at the tops.

From *The Wonderful Wizard of Oz* by L. Frank Baum

Rearrange words to make a sentence

In each sentence below, underline the two words that need to swap places for it to make sense.

1. Although the waiter had recommended different soup, I chose a the dish.

2. The storm began ruined and our picnic was suddenly.

3. We dusted the shelves until scrubbed the floor and it shone.

4. She could whether remember not she had locked the door.

Find the superfluous word

For each question below, make a sentence using all but one of the words. Write the sentence on the line and underline the word that you do not use.

5. his Jason suit in felt accessorise tight-fitting uncomfortable

    _____

6. promptly hammock she back fell leant the in dreaming and asleep

    _____

7. attend that it evening shame is to not to you a will able be this

    _____

8. drifts ideal were covered icicles thick the snow in fields which sledging for

    _____

Complete the word

Add the missing letters to complete the words in the extract below.

9. Matthew s __ __ n t __ r e d leisurely past the f __ __ n __ a __ n. He was not

    due at the o __ __ i c e for another __ o u __ and he p __ a __ n e d to make

    the most of his time by e __ __ l __ r i n g the __ e __ u __ i f __ l park.

In the extract below there are **five** incomplete words. Write the complete words, correctly spelt, on the lines to the right of the box.

10.

The king s __ m __ o __ e d his jester to	i) _____
e __ __ e r __ a __ n him. When the clown	ii) _____
could not be f __ __ __ d, the king pouted and	iii) _____
__ o m __ __ a i __ e d that he was b __ __ e d.	iv) _____
	v) _____

In these questions, you are given a series of numbers. You look for a pattern and find the next number.

Find the next number in the sequence and write it on the line.

2   5   8   11   14   (_____)

First, work out the gap between each number. Write it above.

+3   +3   +3   +3   +3

2   5   8   11   14   (_____)

Then continue the pattern to find the answer.

14 + 3 = 17

Answer: 17

Addition, subtraction and repetition

There are several different pattern types to look out for. Here are the first few with examples.

Adding or subtracting the same number:

−2   −2   −2   −2

11   9   7   5   3

Adding or subtracting an increasing amount:

+1   +2   +3   +4

4   5   7   10   14

Adding or subtracting a decreasing amount:

−5   −4   −3   −2

20   15   11   8   6

Repeating patterns:

+3   +1   +3   +1

6   9   10   13   14   or

+2   +3   +1   +2   +3   +1

7   9   12   13   15   18   19

 Find the next number in the sequence and write it on the line.

1.   8   11   14   17   20   (_____)

2.   25   20   16   13   11   (_____)

3.   12   14   17   19   22   (_____)

4.   18   15   12   9   6   (_____)

5.   28   26   23   22   20   17   (_____)

6.   16   22   27   31   34   (_____)

7.   34   28   23   19   13   8   (_____)

8.   −11   −7   −3   1   5   (_____)

9.   8   11   15   20   26   (_____)

10.   31   30   34   33   37   (_____)

Number sequences

Multiplying and dividing

Here are some more patterns with examples.

Multiply or divide by the same number:

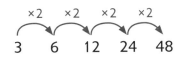

Multiply or divide by an increasing number:

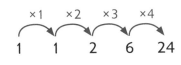

Multiply or divide by a decreasing number:

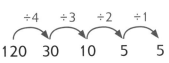

TIP Learn your times tables and the division facts that go with them. For example, if you know that 2 × 4 = 8, then you also know that 4 × 2 = 8, 8 ÷ 4 = 2 and 8 ÷ 2 = 4.

✏️ Find the next number in the sequence and write it on the line.

11. 2 4 8 16 (_____)

12. 160 80 40 20 (_____)

13. 1 3 9 27 (_____)

14. 400 200 100 50 (_____)

15. 5 25 100 300 (_____)

16. 96 48 24 12 (_____)

17. 10 50 200 600 (_____)

18. 1800 300 60 15 (_____)

19. 7 21 63 189 (_____)

20. 1200 120 12 1.2 (_____)

TIP Learn key number facts, such as pairs of numbers that make 10 and 20, halves and doubles, and addition and subtraction facts up to 20. This will help you to spot patterns in number sequences more quickly.

Hidden patterns

Sometimes, the sequences involve patterns that are harder to spot.

You may have to:

- add the previous two numbers

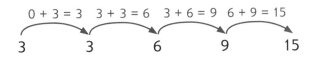

- do two **calculations** ('double **operations**')

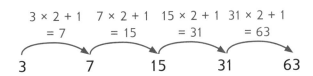

- jump to the next number but one (leapfrogging, as described on page 13). Jump over the last number to get to the answer.

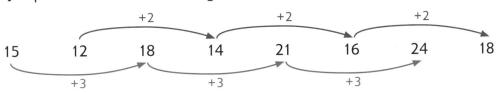

Find the next number in the sequence and write it on the line.

21. 3   2   5   4   7   6   (_____)

22. 30   4   25   8   20   16   (_____)

23. 1   2   3   5   8   (_____)

24. 5   10   15   25   40   (_____)

25. 2   5   11   23   47   (_____)

26. 120   80   60   40   30   20   (_____)

27. 12   12   24   36   60   96   (_____)

28. 4   18   46   102   214   (_____)

29. 1   7   3   14   5   21   7   28   (_____)

30. 2   5   4   10   6   15   (_____)

Squared and cubed numbers

Some sequences contain **squared** or **cubed** numbers.

A squared number is a number multiplied by itself.

For example: $2 \times 2 = 4$, $3 \times 3 = 9$, $4 \times 4 = 16$

4, **9** and **16** are all squared numbers (or 'squares'). Squared numbers are sometimes written like this: $2^2 = 4$, $3^2 = 9$.

A squared numbers sequence might look like this: 4   9   16   25   36
or like this: 81   64   49   36   25.

A cubed number is a number multiplied by itself **twice**.

For example: $2 \times 2 \times 2 = 8$, $3 \times 3 \times 3 = 27$

8 and **27** are both cubed numbers (or 'cubes'). Cubed numbers are sometimes written like this: $2^3 = 8$, $3^3 = 27$.

A cubed numbers sequence might look like this: 27   64   125   216.

TIP It is a good idea to memorise the first few squared and cubed numbers. This will help you to spot patterns in number sequences more quickly.

 Find the next number in the sequence and write it on the line.

31. 27   64   125   216   (_____)

32. 36   49   64   81   (_____)

33. 9   16   25   36   (_____)

34. 216   125   64   27   (_____)

Number sequences

Missing from the beginning

Sometimes, the missing number might be at the beginning of the sequence. Use the same strategies as before to work out the rule by comparing consecutive numbers in the sequence. Then, remember to reverse the rule to find the first number.

Find the missing number in the sequence and write it on the line.

(_____) 8   16   32   64

The rule is double each time so you must do the reverse of this (halve 8), to find the answer.

Answer: 4

 Find the missing number in the sequence and write it on the line.

35. (_____)   20   24   28   32

36. (_____)   9   27   81   243

37. (_____)   5   7   10   14   19

38. (_____)   122   102   82   62

Missing from the middle

Sometimes, the missing numbers are in the middle of the sequence. You then look at the adjacent numbers in order to spot the pattern.

Find the missing number in the sequence and write it on the line.

4   8   13   (_____)   26   34

The jumps increase by one each time. 13 + 6 = 19. The sequence continues with 19 + 7 = 26.

Answer: 19

 Find the missing number in the sequence and write it on the line.

39. 2   4   6   10   (_____)   26

40. 1   3   7   (_____)   31   63

41. 40   8   (_____)   16   20   24   10

42. 5   (_____)   11   17   28   45

In these questions you are given a sum using letters instead of numbers. Using information given, you work out the answer to the sum. You may be asked to write your answer as a letter or as a number.

A = 4, B = 5, C = 6, D = 3, E = 9

What is the answer to this sum, written as a letter?

A + B − C = (_____)

First, write the numbers represented by the letters underneath each letter in the sum.

A + B − C =

4 + 5 − 6 =

Then calculate the answer one step at a time. For tricky sums, write the answer to each step as you go.

4 + 5 = 9 and 9 − 6 = 3

Find the letter that represents your answer.

You know from the information given that D = 3. So, 3 is represented by the letter D.

Answer: D

> (!) Sometimes, instead of a sum, you are given a code. You have to work out the sum of the letters that make up the code by adding them. Look out for some examples in the practice questions.

 Use the information given to answer the sum. Write your answer as a letter.

1.   A = 6, B = 13, C = 5, D = 3, E = 16   D + B = (_____)

2.   A = 10, B = 4, C = 8, D = 20, E = 40   B × A = (_____)

3.   A = 3, B = 13, C = 5, D = 20, E = 15   B + C − E = (_____)

4.   A = 36, B = 6, C = 48, D = 42, E = 8   A ÷ B × E = (_____)

 TIP If your answer is not there, check that you have copied the correct numbers under the letters. Then check each step of the calculation.

Use the set of numbers below to answer the questions that follow. Write your answer as a number.

A = 10, B = 30, C = 24, D = 18, E = 32, F = 8

5.   (B ÷ A) × D − C = (_____)   7.   (A + F) × (C + F) = (_____)

6.   (A × C) − (D + E) = (_____)   8.   F × B ÷ A ÷ C = (_____)

 TIP Remember to work out the answers to the sums in brackets first.

Use the set of numbers below to answer the questions that follow.

A = 12, B = 9, C = 14, D = 16, E = 11, F = 13

9.   Find the sum of the letters in the word FADE.   _____

10.   What is the value of the letters in the word BEAD?   _____

11.   Which three-letter word has a sum of 35?   _____

12.   Which three-letter word has a sum of 40?   _____

Missing number

These questions are often called **equations**. An equation is a number sentence where the two amounts on either side of the equals sign (=) have the same total. The aim is to find the missing number so that the number sentence is correct. The amount on both sides of the equals sign must be the same.

Find the missing number in this equation:

7 + 5 = 20 − (_____)

Calculate the answer to the first half of the equation.

7 + 5 = 12

Work out what number you subtract from 20 to make 12.

You do this by swapping the two halves of the equation.

To find the answer, either count up from 12 to 20 or subtract 12 from 20.

20 − _____ = 12

Answer: 8

> **TIP** Read the question carefully. Do the correct operation. Calculate each step and write your answers as you go.

 Find the missing number in these equations and write it on the line.

1. 6 + 5 = 13 − (_____)

2. 14 − 7 = 2 + (_____)

3. 6 × 3 = 25 − (_____)

4. 25 ÷ 5 = 1 + (_____)

5. 30 − 16 = 7 × (_____)

6. 23 + 41 = 8 × (_____)

7. 18 ÷ 6 = 12 ÷ (_____)

8. 4 × 4 = 2 × (_____)

9. 32 − 12 = 20 + (_____)

10. 11 + 33 = 11 × (_____)

> **TIP** Make sure that you understand the **inverse** operation and how to use it. The inverse of addition is subtraction. The inverse of multiplication is division. (For example, 5 × 6 = 30, 6 × 5 = 30, 30 ÷ 6 = 5, 30 ÷ 5 = 6.)

The level of difficulty of these questions varies. There may be several steps on either side of the equation.

Find the missing number in this equation.

$18 \div 6 + 9 = 3 \times 6 - (\underline{\qquad})$

The technique is as before. Calculate each step separately.

$18 \div 6 = 3$

$3 + 9 = 12$

The first half of the equation equals 12.

Now work out the first step in the second part of the equation.

$3 \times 6 = 18$

Use your findings to write both halves of the equation again.

$12 = 18 - \underline{\qquad}$

Work out what number you subtract from 18 to make 12, or count up from 12 to 18.

Answer: 6

 Find the missing number in these equations and write it on the line.

11. $8 + 14 + 12 = 19 + (\underline{\qquad})$

12. $14 - 7 = 5 + (\underline{\qquad})$

13. $6 \times 3 + 12 = 15 \times (\underline{\qquad})$

14. $40 \div 5 - 2 = 28 - 14 - (\underline{\qquad})$

15. $240 - 50 - 100 = 67 + (\underline{\qquad})$

16. $27 \div 9 \times 100 = 70 \times 3 + (\underline{\qquad})$

17. $4 \times (\underline{\qquad}) = 8 \times 3$

18. $(\underline{\qquad}) - 14 = 56 - 33$

19. $250 \div (\underline{\qquad}) \times 3 = 60 \times 4 - 90$

20. $82 + 62 - (\underline{\qquad}) = 9 \times 9 + 28$

 Where there are several sums within a question, it is usually best to do them in this order:

Brackets (the sum inside the brackets must be answered first, but you can ignore the brackets that show you where to write the answer),

Order (anything to do with the **power** of something, such as 3^2 or 4^3),

Division,

Multiplication,

Addition,

Subtraction.

Remember the **mnemonic: BODMAS**.

Number connections

In number connections questions, there are three sets of numbers. In each set, the middle number is made by carrying out an operation using the two numbers on the outside. You work out what the operation is. Then you find the missing number. It goes in the middle of the third set.

The number in the square brackets is made using the numbers on either side. Work out the missing number and write it on the line.

(4 [12] 3)   (5 [20] 4)   (6 [_____] 5)

Study the first set of numbers. Identify the operation.

(4 [12] 3)

4 × 3 = 12. The operation is multiplication.

Check this works with the second set of numbers.

(5 [20] 4)

5 × 4 = 20. Again, the operation is multiplication.

Apply the same operation to calculate the answer.

(6 [_____] 5)

6 × 5 = 30

Answer: 30

 The calculation used could be addition, subtraction, multiplication or division.

 The number in the square brackets is made using the numbers on either side. Work out the missing number and write it on the line.

1.   (7 [35] 5)   (5 [20] 4)   (4 [_____] 6)

2.   (12 [20] 8)   (14 [21] 7)   (11 [_____] 9)

3.   (23 [20] 3)   (31 [23] 8)   (25 [_____] 6)

4.   (5 [40] 8)   (4 [12] 3)   (5 [_____] 3)

5.   (4 [10] 40)   (10 [10] 100)   (9 [_____] 36)

6.   (6 [24] 4)   (11 [44] 4)   (7 [_____] 8)

7.   (54 [6] 9)   (48 [8] 6)   (72 [_____] 9)

8.   (36 [15] 21)   (45 [23] 22)   (65 [_____] 24)

These questions may involve two steps or operations.

 TIP Learning your multiplication and division facts will help you to answer these questions more quickly.

The number in the square brackets is made using the numbers on either side. Work out the missing number and write it on the line.

(6 [30] 9)   (4 [20] 6)   (3 [_____] 5)

(6 [30] 9)   (4 [20] 6)   (3 [?] 5)   Call the number on the left **a**, the one on the
(**a** [**c**] **b**) ◄─────────────────────── right **b** and the one in the middle **c**. In the first
set of numbers, **a** is **6**, **b** is **9** and **c** is **30**.

Study the first set of numbers. Identify the most likely first step.

(6 [30] 9)   The middle number [**c**] is bigger, so the operation is likely to be addition
or multiplication.

Choose an operation to try out first.

(6 [30] 9)   Try addition: 6 + 9 = 15.

But **c** is 30. How could you get from 15 to 30?

There are two possibilities for the second step: 15 + 15 = 30 **or**
15 × 2 = 30.

These may be shown as **a** + **b** + 15 **or** (**a** + **b**) × 2.

Test your chosen operation with the other set of numbers given:

(4 [20] 6)   The first step is **a** + **b**. 4 + 6 = 10.

For the second step, try + 15. But 10 + 15 = 25, not 20.
So, this second step is wrong.

Try the alternative step, × 2. 10 × 2 = 20.   **TIP** If you do not find
So, the two steps are (**a** + **b**) × 2.   the answer first
time, try again

Finally, apply these two steps (**a** + **b**) × 2 to the third set of numbers: with a different
first step.
(3 [_____] 5)   3 + 5 = 8; 8 × 2 = 16.   **Answer: 16**

First step

The first step is usually addition, subtraction, multiplication or division using the two numbers on the outside (**a** and **b**). Carry out the first step.

Second step

Work out how you get from that answer to the number in the middle [**c**].   **TIP** There are
sometimes
The most common second steps are: variations
to the steps

- add one of the numbers on either side (+ **a** or + **b**)   shown above.
The steps
- subtract one of the numbers on either side (− **a** or − **b**)   described here
are the most
- add or subtract a random number (+ **z** or − **z**)   common.

- double (× 2) or halve (÷ 2).

110

Try both steps

Make a note of the two operations, then try them with the second set of numbers. If the same steps work for both sets, use these steps with the third set of numbers to find your answer. If not, try a different first step.

 The number in the square brackets is made using the numbers on either side. Work out the missing number and write it on the line.

9. (2 [20] 5)   (5 [40] 4)   (4 [_____] 6)

10. (6 [10] 3)   (12 [18] 5)   (21 [_____] 5)

11. (4 [7] 12)   (3 [11] 15)   (5 [_____] 20)

12. (16 [12] 8)   (15 [9] 3)   (14 [_____] 10)

13. (12 [14] 3)   (15 [13] 5)   (24 [_____] 6)

14. (21 [16] 38)   (12 [29] 42)   (16 [_____] 32)

15. (63 [16] 9)   (56 [15] 7)   (72 [_____] 9)

16. (12 [18] 14)   (28 [42] 22)   (35 [_____] 34)

> **TIP** Try the operation that looks most likely first. Check that the same operations work with both sample sets.

Sometimes, these questions may be expressed using words.

Work out the missing number and write it on the line.

(6 is to 18)   (4 is to 12)   (8 is to _____)

> Use the same strategies as before, this time working out the relationship between the two numbers in the first two sets of brackets and applying the same rule to find the missing number in the third set of brackets. In this example, 6 is multiplied by 3 to make 18 and 4 is multiplied by 3 to make 12. To find the answer, multiply 8 by 3, which makes 24. So, the answer is 24.
>
> **Answer:** (6 is to 18)   (4 is to 12)   (8 is to __24__)

 Work out the missing number and write it on the line.

17. (12 is to 6)   (24 is to 12)   (34 is to _____)

18. (21 is to 31)   (45 is to 55)   (93 is to _____)

19. (120 is to 30)   (84 is to 21)   (72 is to _____)

20. (144 is to 12)   (36 is to 6)   (64 is to _____)

21. (350 is to 35)   (45 is to 4.5)   (108 is to _____)

22. (44 is to 33)   (76 is to 65)   (108 is to _____)

23. (13 is to 39)   (12 is to 36)   (14 is to _____)

24. (33 is to 2)   (55 is to 4)   (88 is to _____)

Now test your skills with these practice pages. If you get stuck, go back to pages 102 to 111 for some reminders.

Number sequences

Find the missing number in the sequence and write it on the line.

1. 7 14 21 28 35 (_____)

2. 6 12 24 48 96 (_____)

3. 96 84 72 60 48 (_____)

4. 9 16 25 36 49 (_____)

5. 8 10 14 20 28 (_____)

6. 9 54 18 48 27 42 (_____)

7. 4 9 19 39 79 (_____)

8. 12 24 36 60 96 (_____)

9. 480 240 120 60 (_____)

10. 1 8 27 64 (_____)

11. (_____) 6 30 120 360 720

12. 5 11 23 (_____) 95 191

13. 20000 (_____) 200 20 2 0.2

14. 48 108 36 96 24 (_____) 12

15. (_____) 93 53 33 23 18

Letters for numbers

In these questions, letters stand for numbers. Use the information given to answer the sum. Write your answer as a letter.

16. A = 9, B = 12, C = 15, D = 2, E = 14   D + B = (_____)

17. A = 7, B = 4, C = 28, D = 26, E = 21   B × A = (_____)

18. A = 3, B = 5, C = 7, D = 15, E = 9   B + C − E = (_____)

19. A = 19, B = 23, C = 15, D = 2, E = 27   (C + B) ÷ A = (_____)

20. A = 3, B = 60, C = 5, D = 4, E = 75   A × D × C = (_____)

21. A = 7, B = 66, C = 17, D = 31, E = 73   C + (A × A) = (_____)

22. A = 9, B = −8, C = −4, D = −5, E = 8   D + A − E = (_____)

23. A = 21, B = 12, C = 54, D = 6, E = 27   C ÷ D + B = (_____)

24. A = 8, B = 54, C = 5, D = 24, E = 14   B − (A × C) = (_____)

25. A = 84, B = 6, C = 12, D = 72, E = 42
     Find the total of the letters in the word BEAD. _____

26. A = 40, B = 26, C = 34, D = 37, E = 29, F = 21
     What is the value of the letters in the word FEED? _____

27. A = 28, B = 18, C = 3, D = 24, E = 14
     Deduct the value of the letters in the word BAD from the sum of the letters in the word ADD.

     _____

Missing number

Find the missing number in these equations and write it on the line.

1. $11 + 24 = 40 - ($_____$)$

2. $34 - 12 = 15 + ($_____$)$

3. $7 \times 8 = 20 + ($_____$)$

4. $81 \div 9 = 3 \times ($_____$)$

5. $40 - 21 = 17 + ($_____$)$

6. $160 \div 4 = 7 \times 6 - ($_____$)$

7. $71 + 20 - 16 = 9 \times 4 + ($_____$)$

8. $6 \times 6 + 4 = 120 \div ($_____$)$

9. $84 \times 2 + 30 = 101 + ($_____$)$

10. $74 - 51 + 12 = 38 - ($_____$)$

11. $12 \times ($_____$) - 8 = 15 \times 4 + 16$

12. $36 \div 4 \times 3 + ($_____$) = 11 \times 7 - 42$

13. $($_____$) \times 7 - 9 = 3 \times 8 + 9$

14. $($_____$) \div 7 + 19 - 6 = 2 \times 32 - 40 - 4$

15. $(4^2 \times 2) \div 4 = 77 \div 11 + ($_____$)$

Number connections

The number in the square brackets is made using the numbers on either side. Work out the missing number and write it on the line.

16. (3 [24] 8)   (6 [54] 9)   (7 [_____] 6)

17. (16 [28] 12)   (19 [32] 13)   (15 [_____] 18)

18. (45 [30] 15)   (54 [32] 22)   (73 [_____] 26)

19. (72 [8] 9)   (48 [6] 8)   (110 [_____] 10)

20. (13 [16] 29)   (52 [11] 63)   (46 [_____] 84)

21. (16 [20] 8)   (27 [30] 9)   (40 [_____] 5)

22. (12 [35] 3)   (6 [65] 11)   (4 [_____] 7)

23. (24 [51] 37)   (43 [67] 34)   (21 [_____] 19)

24. (35 [49] 7)   (53 [77] 12)   (43 [_____] 14)

25. (88 [26] 75)   (96 [86] 53)   (62 [_____] 39)

26. (29 [11] 4)   (6 [22] 60)   (15 [_____] 21)

27. (45 [8] 61)   (18 [9] 36)   (58 [_____] 96)

Work out the missing number and write it on the line.

28. (6 is to 18)   (7 is to 21)   (9 is to _____)

29. (96 is to 24)   (140 is to 35)   (212 is to _____)

Number logic

In problem-solving questions, you read some information and use this to answer a question.

Number logic questions test your reading and mental arithmetic skills. You are given a statement and you must identify the number being described.

Identify the number being described. Write your answer on the line.

This number is four times bigger than half of ten. _____

Read the statement carefully. Decide what arithmetic you need to do in order to identify the number.

Start by finding half of ten, then multiply the answer by four to find the answer. Half of ten is five. Five multiplied by four is twenty.

Answer: This number is four times bigger than half of ten. _____**twenty**_____

It often helps to work backwards from the number you are given.

Identify the number being described. Write your answer on the line.

If I halve this number and then quarter the answer, I get six. _____

Start by finding six times four, then double the number to find the answer.

Six times four is twenty-four. Twenty-four doubled is forty-eight.

Answer: If I halve this number and then quarter the answer, I get six. _____**forty-eight**_____

For each question below, identify the number being described. Write your answer on the line.

1. If I double this number and subtract six, the answer is twenty-two. _____

2. This number is three less than a third of thirty-six. _____

3. Fifteen is half as big as triple this number. _____

4. Adding eight to this number makes it sixteen less than seventy-two. _____

5. If I subtract eleven from half of this number, the answer is fourteen. _____

6. If I double this number and then triple the answer, I get six. _____

7. A third of twenty-seven is a fifth of this number. _____

8. This number is twelve less than double nineteen. _____

9. Forty-eight is twice as big as a third of this number. _____

10. If I add twenty-three to a quarter of this number, the answer is thirty-one. _____

Schofield & Sims

Days and dates

Dates questions involve reading some information and using this to identify a day of the week or a month of the year.

It is very important that you read all the information you are given before trying to answer.

What day was it the day before yesterday if tomorrow is Saturday?

Write the days of the week in their shortened forms.

M T W Th F Sa Su

Establish what day today is.

If tomorrow is Saturday, today must be Friday, so put your finger on Friday.

Point to the days as you work through the problem.

If today is Friday, yesterday must have been Thursday, so the day **before** Thursday would have been Wednesday.

Answer: ___**Wednesday**___

TIP For questions involving months, write them in shortened form:
Ja Fe Mar Ap May Jun Jul Au Se Oc No De

For each question below, identify the day or month being described. Write your answer on the line.

1. If tomorrow is Sunday, what day was it yesterday? _____

2. Sam's brother was born in September, three months before his friend, Jack, who was born a month after Stephen. In which month was Stephen born? _____

3. If it is going to be Saturday in three days' time, what day is it today? _____

4. My birthday party took place four days after my birthday, which was on a Wednesday. What day was my party? _____

5. What month are we in now if last month was two months after Christmas? _____

6. If next month is May, what month was it the month before last? _____

TIP Make sure that you know key facts off by heart: the days in each month, the hours in a day, the weeks in a year. This will help you to answer days and dates questions more quickly.

Some questions involve working out a specific date.

If 5th September is a Monday, what day is 9th November?

Think which months are between September and November.
October comes between these two months.

Jot down the number of days in September and October.
September: 30 days. October: 31 days.

Count on from 5th September to find the dates of all the Mondays.
There are seven days in a week, so by adding sevens you can work out all the Monday dates:
5th, 12th, 19th, 26th September.

As you reach late September, count on in ones to the end of the month.
When you get to 30th September, start again from one.
Tues 27th Sept, Weds 28th Sept, Thurs 29th Sept, Fri 30th Sept, Sat 1st Oct, Sun 2nd Oct.
3rd October is the first Monday in October.

Add seven to each date to find the other Mondays in October.
10th, 17th, 24th, 31st October

There are 31 days in October, so count on seven more days to find the first Monday in November.
The first Monday in November is 7th November.

7th November is a Monday.
9th November is two days after Monday, so it is a Wednesday.

Answer: ___**Wednesday**___

✏️ Work out the answer to the question and write it on the line.

7. If 2nd January is a Saturday, what day is 30th January? _____

8. In a leap year, 1st February falls on a Monday. How many Wednesdays would there be in March? _____

9. If 5th August is a Sunday, what day was 25th July? _____

10. How many Wednesdays are there in September if the last day of the month is a Tuesday? _____

11. What date is the last Friday in April if 25th March is a Thursday? _____

12. How many days after Halloween is Christmas Day? _____

Time

Time questions are often best solved using a table.

Zara leaves for work 30 minutes after Melody, who has a 40-minute journey. Melody arrives at work at 9.15 a.m. Aisha takes 25 minutes to get to work and arrives 10 minutes after Skye, who gets in at 8.30 a.m. Emily leaves for work at the same time as Zara and has a journey the same length as Melody. What time does Emily arrive at work?

Read all the information. Think carefully about what the question is asking.

Draw a simple table. Re-read the information. Add to the table any definite facts (shown in black below).

Work out the rest of the information.

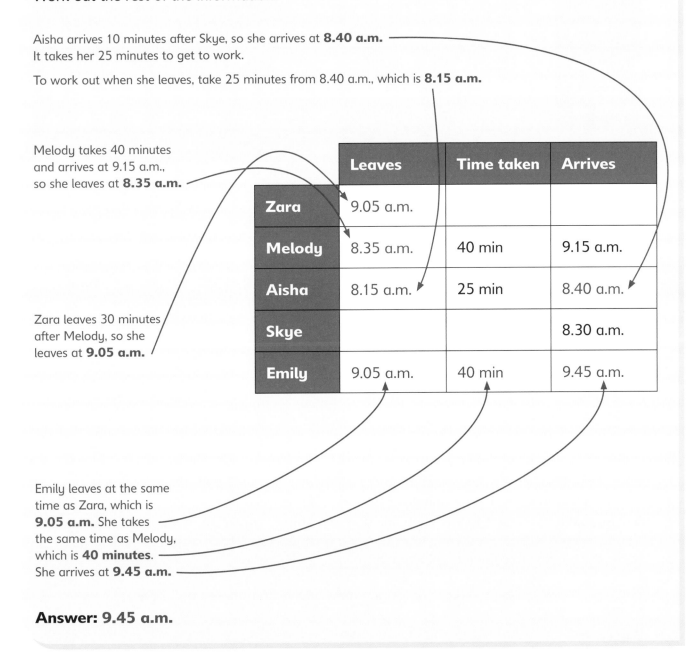

Aisha arrives 10 minutes after Skye, so she arrives at **8.40 a.m.**
It takes her 25 minutes to get to work.

To work out when she leaves, take 25 minutes from 8.40 a.m., which is **8.15 a.m.**

Melody takes 40 minutes and arrives at 9.15 a.m., so she leaves at **8.35 a.m.**

Zara leaves 30 minutes after Melody, so she leaves at **9.05 a.m.**

	Leaves	**Time taken**	**Arrives**
Zara	9.05 a.m.		
Melody	8.35 a.m.	40 min	9.15 a.m.
Aisha	8.15 a.m.	25 min	8.40 a.m.
Skye			8.30 a.m.
Emily	9.05 a.m.	40 min	9.45 a.m.

Emily leaves at the same time as Zara, which is **9.05 a.m.** She takes the same time as Melody, which is **40 minutes**. She arrives at **9.45 a.m.**

Answer: 9.45 a.m.

Now answer the following questions.

1. Pratik, Callum, Prianka and Chrissy all have to be at school by 9 a.m. Pratik catches the 8.20 a.m. bus outside his house and arrives at school 10 minutes early. Prianka leaves home at 8.35 a.m. and has a 20-minute walk. Callum leaves home five minutes before Prianka and arrives five minutes after her. Chrissy has a 15-minute cycle ride to school and arrives five minutes before Callum. What time does Chrissy leave home?

   Use the table below to work out your answer.

	Leaves	Time taken	Arrives
Pratik			
Callum			
Prianka			
Chrissy			

   Answer: _____

2. Salima, Rafi and Emmanuel each take less than two hours to complete their homework. Salima starts at 4.05 p.m., half an hour before Rafi, and finishes at 5.45 p.m. Rafi takes an hour and a half and finishes 20 minutes after Emmanuel, who starts at 5 p.m. How long does Emmanuel's homework take?

   Draw your own table on a piece of rough paper. Write the answer below.

   Answer: _____

3. Four snails have a race. Brian sets off at 1.25 p.m. and takes 32 minutes to complete the course. Sheldon sets off eight minutes after Brian but completes the course in half the time. Sidney takes 12 minutes longer than Sheldon and finishes at 2.22 p.m. Brenda sets off one minute before Sheldon and completes the course at the same time as Brian. Which snail takes the longest to complete the course?

   Draw your own table on a piece of rough paper and write the answer below.

   Answer: _____

In these questions you work out where one thing is in relation to another. Drawing a diagram helps you to use the information you are given.

Four children are having a picnic. They sit one on each side of a rectangular rug and face the middle. Amita is not sitting next to Megan, who is to the left of Jasmine. Paige is sitting opposite Jasmine.

Who is sitting to the right of Paige?

Draw a rectangle to represent the rug. Then put the girls in place, using short forms of their names.

Start by placing Amita in any position and then work from there.

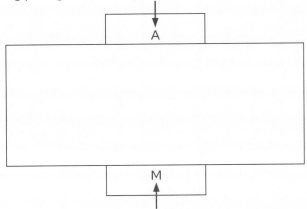

Since Amita is not sitting next to Megan, you know she is sitting opposite her.
So you can put Megan in place.

You also know that Megan is to the left of Jasmine. The girls are sitting facing the middle, so Jasmine has to be to the right of Megan.

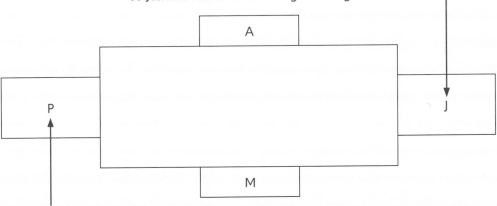

Finally, you can put Paige into the last position.
Now you can see that Megan is sitting to the right of Paige.

 TIP Play with the information given. If necessary, use **trial and error** until you find the answer.

Answer: _____ **Megan** _____

Position

 Use the pictures and lines beneath each question to help you position your answers.

1. Five friends, Barney, Jasper, Harry, Vanessa and Shannon, live in a row on Hart Street. Harry lives between Barney and Jasper, who also lives next to Shannon. Vanessa lives at one end of the street, next door to Barney.

   Who lives at the other end of the street? _____

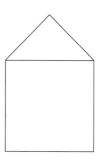 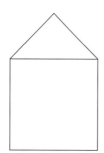  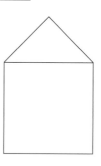 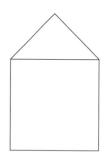

2. Seven people are in a queue at a bus stop. Riley is in front of Lily but behind Brooke. Brooke is behind Tegan who is behind Umar. Julian is behind Lily. Maxwell is at the back of the queue.

   Who is at the front of the queue? _____

   back of the queue   *front of the queue*

   _____ _____ _____ _____ _____ _____ _____

3. Five children, Theo, Kaiden, Darcie, Faye and Lois, are holding hands in a circle, facing inwards. Theo is holding hands with Darcie and Lois, who is not holding hands with Faye.

   Which **two** children is Faye holding hands with?

   _____ and _____

   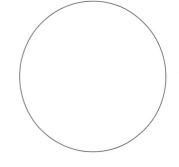

TIP When you make a chart to solve a problem, using shortened forms of names and other details saves you time.

4. Poppy, Mia, Troy, Lee and Milly are queuing for the bus. Mia is between Milly and Troy, who is at the back. Poppy is behind Lee.

   Who is at the front? _____

   _____ _____ _____ _____ _____

5. Five children – Lucy, Maddy, Jose, Taylor and Nathan – are sitting around a circular table. Lucy is to the right of Maddy who is not next to Nathan. Jose is in between Nathan and Lucy.

   Who is to the left of Maddy? _____

   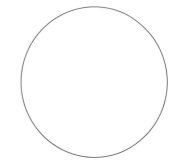

Sorting information

These questions can often be solved by drawing a table.

Jamie, Hannah, Mohammed, Samira and Tamara all like to play sport. Jamie enjoys rugby, football and cricket but does not like swimming. Hannah enjoys netball, football and swimming. Mohammed likes swimming, football, rugby and cricket. Samira likes everything except rugby. Tamara likes football, swimming and cricket. How many children like swimming?

Read the information given carefully. Think about what the question is asking.

Draw a table and use the information to complete it.

	Ru	Fo	Cr	Sw	Ne
Ja	/	/	/	✗	
Ha		/		/	/
Mo	/	/	/	/	
Sa	✗	/	/	/	/
Ta		/	/	/	

Re-read the information, one bit at a time.

Fill in the table, using a tally system to note each fact.

Check the **Sw** column to see how many children like swimming.

Answer: 4

 Now answer the following questions.

1. Five children order an ice-cream sundae each. Max has vanilla, chocolate and strawberry ice-cream in his. Molly has vanilla, fudge and banana. Alex has raspberry ripple, chocolate, banana and a scoop of fudge. Susie has only fudge. Faiz has banana, chocolate and fudge How many children have both banana and fudge?

	Ch	Ba	Fu	Va	St	Ra
Ma						
Mo						
Al						
Su						
Fa						

Answer: _____

2. A cat has six kittens. Two of them have brown stripes and white paws. One of them has black paws and no stripes. One is black with three white paws and one black paw. One of them has grey stripes and white paws. One of them is white all over.

How many white paws are there altogether? **Answer:** _____

3. A group of friends wrap up warmly to play in the snow. Alice wears a pink bobble hat and gloves. Boris wears a scarf and gloves. Cameron wears a hat and a scarf but no gloves. Dottie wears gloves, a scarf and a hat. Ella has a cold so she stays inside. Florence wears a scarf and gloves.

How many children wear at least two items of extra clothing?

Fill in the table to find the answer.

Answer: _____

4. At the Music Academy, pupils can choose up to four different instruments to play. Ajay plays the flute, violin and cello. Leena plays the piano, harp and cello. Amy plays the piano, violin, flute and saxophone. Robert plays the guitar, piano and flute. Yan plays the flute, cello, piano and harp. Beth used to play the harp but now she plays the flute and violin.

How many children play both the piano and flute?

Draw your own table on a piece of rough paper and write the answer below.

Answer: _____

5. Ollie is sorting some parcels at the post office. Parcel A weighs 500g more than parcel B, which is 0.75kg lighter than parcel C. Parcel C weighs 1.5kg. Parcel D is double the weight of parcel B.

How much does parcel D weigh? _____

A	B	C	D

122

In these questions, you are given one or more true statements. You are then given five more statements, **A** to **E**, which are either true or false. You are asked to identify either the one true statement or the one false statement that you can deduce from the information you are given.

If the statements shown in **bold** are true, which **one** of the statements listed beneath them is also true?

Carrots are a root vegetable.

Root vegetables grow underground.

A.   Carrots are orange.

B.   All trees have roots.

C.   Carrots grow underground.

D.   Rabbits like carrots.

E.   All vegetables grow underground.

Read through the first statements, thinking carefully about what they are telling you.

Next, read statements **A** to **E**. Compare them to the information given. Decide whether they are true.

A.   Carrots are orange.   True, but you **cannot** deduce this from the statements given.

B.   All trees have roots.   True, but you **cannot** deduce this from the statements given.

C.   Carrots grow underground.   True, and you **can** deduce this from the statements given.

Answer: C

 Sometimes, you may be asked to identify **two** statements that are true, or perhaps the one statement that is **not** true. Always make sure you read the question carefully to check what you are being asked to find.

 Now answer the following questions.

If the statements shown in **bold** are true, which **one** of the statements listed beneath them is also true?

1.   **Bananas are yellow.**

   Bananas are a type of fruit.

   A.   Bananas are tasty.

   B.   All yellow fruit grows on trees.

   C.   Bananas are a yellow fruit.

   D.   All fruit is yellow.

   E.   Monkeys like bananas.

   Answer: _____

If the statements shown in **bold** are true, which **one** of the statements listed beneath them is also true?

2. **Eagles are birds of prey.**

   Birds of prey hunt for their food.

   A. Eagles are covered in feathers.

   B. Eagles hunt for their food.

   C. All birds are eagles.

   D. All eagles have wings.

   E. Eagles' beaks are yellow.

   Answer: _____

3. **Cars are a form of transport.**

   Forms of transport move us from place to place.

   A. All forms of transport have wheels.

   B. Lorries are forms of transport.

   C. Cars move us from place to place.

   D. Cars have wheels.

   E. Cars carry luggage.

   Answer: _____

4. **Summer is a season.**

   There are four seasons.

   A. Winter is a season.

   B. People eat ice lollies in the summer.

   C. Summer is hot.

   D. Christmas is in winter.

   E. Summer is one of four seasons.

   Answer: _____

5. **Oranges are a type of citrus fruit.**

   Citrus fruit grows on trees.

   A. Orange juice is a type of drink.

   B. Orange juice is tasty.

   C. Oranges are sticky.

   D. Oranges grow on trees.

   E. All fruit grow on trees.

   Answer: _____

If the statements shown in **bold** are true, which **one** of the statements listed beneath them is **not** true?

6. **Alistair offers his friends some fruit from the fruit bowl.**

   Daisy chooses a banana or a pear.

   Zack only likes apples and bananas.

   Rebecca prefers apples but she will also eat bananas and pears.

   Edward doesn't eat any fruit.

   A. Rebecca likes all the fruit.

   B. Rebecca eats an apple.

   C. Edward doesn't eat bananas.

   D. Zack doesn't like pears.

   E. Daisy doesn't eat bananas or pears.

   Answer: _____

Now test your skills with these practice pages. If you get stuck, go back to pages 114 to 124 for some reminders.

Number logic

For each question below, identify the number being described. Write your answer on the line.

1. If I halve this number, the answer is a quarter of 28. _____

2. Subtracting nine from this number makes it seventeen more than 51. _____

3. 30 is twice as big as triple this number. _____

4. If I add this number to itself, I get the product of six and seven. _____

5. Adding a fifth of forty-five to this number makes a third of sixty-six. _____

6. This number is less than double twenty-nine but more than half of one hundred and twelve. _____

Days and dates

For each question below, identify the day or month being described. Write your answer on the line.

7. Juliette is five months older than Martha, who was born the month before Neema. If Neema was born in June, in which month was Juliette born? _____

8. Stanley's older brother, Freddie, went on a trip round the world for 18 months. He returned home in March. In which month did he set off? _____

9. Today is Tuesday 22nd May. I am going on holiday on the third Thursday in June. What date will this be? _____

Time

Answer the following questions. Write your answer on the line.

10. Toby is waiting for his flight from London to New York. It was due to depart at 08:35 but is 20 minutes late. The flight takes eight hours. The time in New York is five hours behind the UK. What time will it be in New York when the plane arrives? _____

11. Rhys' alarm clock goes off at 7.30 a.m. but it is five minutes fast. When the alarm goes off, Rhys hits the snooze button. He goes back to sleep for 15 minutes. It takes Rhys 25 minutes to get to school. If he is due in school at 8.45 a.m., how long does he have to get ready and still be on time? _____

12. I am making a pizza. It takes 35 minutes to prepare the dough and then I must leave it to rise for 25 minutes. Once the dough has risen, it will take me 10 minutes to add the sauce and toppings. The pizza will take 15 minutes to cook. I have guests arriving at 19:45 and I want the pizza to be ready 5 minutes after they arrive. What time should I start making the pizza? _____

Position

Answer the following questions. Write your answer on the line.

1. Sashika, Maya, Bilal, Chloe, Sakshay and Joel are queuing for lunch. Maya is in front of Chloe but two behind Sakshay, who is in front of Joel. Bilal is not at the back but is further back than Chloe. Who is first? _____

2. Helen is sorting out her parcels at the post office. Parcel A weighs 1.5kg, which is 750g heavier than parcel C but 0.25kg lighter than Parcel B. Parcel D weighs 150g more than parcel A and 50g less than parcel E. How much does the lightest parcel weigh? _____

3. Mae was hiking up a mountain with her five friends. Tina was at the front but she stopped for a rest and was overtaken by everybody else. Louisa was ahead of Mae but behind Frances who was second from the front. Zoe was in front of Frances. Who was Serena behind? _____

Sorting information

Answer the following questions. Write your answer on the line.

4. In the burger bar, you can choose any of these toppings: cheese, gherkins, chilli, lettuce, relish and tomatoes. Savi had all the toppings except relish. Bethany and Jordan had cheese, chilli and gherkins on their burgers. Malcolm is allergic to cheese but had everything else apart from chilli. Rhianna had the same as Savi. Angela had a plain burger. How many toppings did the children have altogether? _____

5. There are six cars in a car park. Cars **A** and **D** are saloons. Car **E** is a saloon with red stripes and blue doors. Cars **B** and **C** are hatchbacks; one is green and the other is black. Car **F** is a red estate car with black stripes. All the saloons and one of the hatchbacks have a sunroof. All the cars with stripes have air conditioning. How many cars have both a sunroof and air conditioning? _____

6. Peter had a bag of 100 marbles. He gave some to his friends. He gave 12 more to Archie than he gave to Isla, who had half as many as Susan. Saul was given 18, which was two more than Susan, but he lost three under the sofa. Mark received a third of the number Saul was given. How many marbles did Peter have left? _____

Archie	Isla	Susan	Saul	Mark

True statements

If the statements shown in **bold** are true, which **one** of the statements listed beneath them is also true?

1. **Crabs are a type of crustacean.**

   All crustaceans have hard outer shells.

   A. Crabs have pincers.

   B. All crustaceans are crabs.

   C. Crabs have a hard outer shell.

   D. Crabs live in the sea.

   E. Crabs look like spiders.

   Answer: _____

2. **Paper is often made from wood.**

   Wood comes from trees.

   A. Paper is for writing on.

   B. Books are made out of paper.

   C. Furniture is made out of wood.

   D. Paper can be made from trees.

   E. Paper is white.

   Answer: _____

If the statements shown in **bold** are true, which **one** of the statements listed beneath them is **not** true?

3. **Luke is older than Miles but younger than Jake.**

   Stella is two months older than Tristan.

   Django is two years younger than Miles and six months older than Tristan.

   Marv is Jake's twin brother.

   A. Luke is not the oldest.

   B. Stella is younger than Django.

   C. Stella is the youngest.

   D. Marv is the same age as Jake.

   E. Tristan is younger than Stella.

   Answer: _____

4. **During the summer break, four friends from London are all going on holiday.**

   Marc is going camping in Wales for a week.

   Sheena is caravanning in France for two weeks.

   Mattie will be staying in a villa in Spain for three weeks.

   Puja is going glamping in Devon for a fortnight.

   A. Sheena and Puja will be away for the same length of time.

   B. Puja and Marc will be staying in tents.

   C. Marc's holiday was more expensive than Sheena's.

   D. Mattie is not going abroad.

   E. The weather in France is better than the weather in Wales.

   Answer: _____

Parents' notes

This book is divided into seven sections, representing seven key areas tested in 11+ verbal reasoning exams:

- word and letter patterns
- vocabulary
- grammar
- spelling
- cloze
- number patterns
- problem-solving

Each section contains explanations of verbal reasoning question types, as well as sets of practice questions. The book can therefore be worked through in its entirety, or you may select particular sections for your child to focus on.

If your child is sitting an 11+ exam set by CEM, the verbal reasoning sections of their exam may include some comprehension questions. They will be asked to read a passage and answer some questions about it. Explanations and examples of comprehension questions can be found in the **11+ English Study and Practice Book**, which is also available from Schofield & Sims.

Administering the Practice test

- When your child is confident answering each question type, they should sit the Practice test. This should be done in exam conditions, with an adult timing and marking the test.

- Before beginning the test, make sure your child has a pencil, an eraser and a sheet of rough paper. Also ensure that your child is able to see a clock or a watch.

- Advise your child to read each question carefully.

- Answers need to be written clearly. In some 11+ exams your child will be asked to rub out an incorrect answer, but in others they will be asked to cross it out. Explain to your child what to do if they make a mistake.

- Encourage your child to check their answers if they have time at the end of the test. This will also allow them to make sure that they haven't accidentally missed out any questions.

- The Practice test is divided by question type to allow you to identify any areas that your child has not yet understood.

- There is a time limit of 1 hour. When your child has finished the test, you should mark it using the answers section of this book. There are 142 marks available in total.

- The table below will help you to plan the next steps. However, these are suggestions only. Please use your own judgement as you decide how best to proceed.

Score	Time taken	Target met?	Action
1–114	Any	Not yet	Work through the explanation sections of this book again, ensuring that all question types are understood. If your child struggled with particular question types in the Practice test, focus on those sections.
115–142	Over the target – child took too long	Not yet	Use the appropriate age level **11+ Verbal Reasoning Rapid Tests** to improve speed.
115–142	On target – child took suggested time or less	Yes	Move on to **11+ Verbal Reasoning Rapid Tests** or **Progress Papers** to continue developing speed, accuracy and skill.

For further guidance on 11+ verbal reasoning exams, download the free **Parents' Guide to the 11+** from the **Schofield & Sims** website. This provides an overview of the exams and contains useful advice on organising your child's revision, as well as how to help them prepare for the day of the exam.

Practice test

Alphabet positions

Use the alphabet to help you answer the questions below.

A B C D E F G H I J K L M N O P Q R S T U V W X Y Z

1.   Which letter is at position 19 in the alphabet?   ____

2.   If the letters that spell **FREEDOM** were removed from the alphabet, which letter would
     be in position 10 of the new alphabet?   ____

3.   Find the letter that appears twice in **PERMISSIBLE**, once in **SILAGE** and twice
     in **SILENCE**.   ____

Alphabetical order

Use the alphabet above to help you answer the questions below.

4.   If the letters in the word **CAVERNOUS** are arranged in alphabetical order, which letter
     comes in the middle?   ____

5.   If these words were placed in alphabetical order, which word would be fifth in the list?

     atoned   attest   attire   attempt   atomic   attract   _____

Letter sequences

Using the alphabet above to help you, find the missing pair of letters in each series.

6.   BD CE DF EG FH (___ ___)

7.   JL HI FF DC BZ (___ ___)

Letter codes

Find the letters that complete the sentence in the best way. Use the alphabet above to help you.

8.   **FX** is to **UC** as **JE** is to?   ____ ____

9.   **SN** is to **WH** as **YG** is to?   ____ ____

Word codes

Work out the code or word for each question below. Use the alphabet above to help you.

10. If the code for **LAUGHED** is **OCVJJFG**, what is **SMILES** in code?   _____

11. If the code for **HEALTH** is ¬∪●∈∧¬, what does ∈●∧¬∪ mean?   _____

12. If **GENTLER** in code is **TVMGOVI**, what is the code for **HOSTILE**?   _____

/12

Match the codes

Match the number codes to the words below. Then answer the questions.

R U N T   R A S H   H U G S   H E N S

     3 7 6 8   4 7 1 9   4 5 8 3

13. What are the codes for:

    i)   **GASH**? _____   **ii)**   **STUNG**? _____

Make a word from one other word

In these questions there are three pairs of words. The third pair of words is made in the same way as the first two pairs. Find the missing word and write it on the line.

14. (demean mend)   (easier sire)   (harass _____)

15. (breeze beer)   (recite rice)   (strong _____)

Make a word from two other words

In these questions, the word in the middle of the second group is made in the same way as the word in the middle of the first group. Find the word that is missing in the second group and write it on the line.

16. (built [dial] aside)   (deeds [_____] event)

17. (office [fairy] starry)   (access [_____] scream)

Word meanings

Read each sentence and then answer the questions that follow.

The deeply pious minister prayed daily.

18. What does 'pious' mean?

    A. envious   **B.** occasional   **C.** religious   **D.** emotional   **E.** furtive   ____

Having bought the artwork on a whim, she now regretted her impulsiveness.

19. What does 'whim' mean?

    A. discounted   **B.** estuary   **C.** gallery   **D.** demand   **E.** urge   ____

/8

Sort words into groups

A	B	C	D
quail	orchid	downpour	plaster
lark	gerbera	cyclone	concrete
kite	chrysanthemum	drought	marble
heron	allium	typhoon	granite

20. Look at the words below. Which group in the table (**A**, **B**, **C** or **D**) does each of them belong to? Choose the correct letter and write it on the line.

i)   cement   ____

ii) buzzard   ____

iii) dandelion   ____

iv) monsoon   ____

v)   snowdrop   ____

vi) blizzard   ____

Ordering words

Put these words in sequence from smallest to largest, then identify the word in the middle.

21. country   town   village   continent   county   _____

22. sparrow   ostrich   swan   raven   chicken   _____

23. tetrahedron   sphere   cuboid   cylinder   cone   _____

Synonyms

Underline the **two** words, **one** from each group, that are most similar in meaning.

24. (ordinary aristocracy ability)   (nobility remarkable temporary)

Underline the word in brackets that is closest in meaning to the word in capitals.

25. EVENTUALLY   (occasionally, frequently, ultimately, basically, fully)

Add the missing letters to make a word that is similar in meaning to the word in capitals.

26. CONTROL   r __ s __ __ a __ n

/12

Antonyms

Underline the pair of words that is most opposite in meaning.

27. (affix, detach)   (tempt, convince)   (rehearse, audition)

Find the word that is opposite in meaning to the word in capitals and that rhymes with the word in italics.

28. VANISH   *sphere*   _____

Add the missing letters to make a word that is opposite in meaning to the word in capitals.

29. SINGULAR   __ l __ r a __

Synonym and antonym grid

30. Use the grid to answer the questions below.

energetic	criticise	mean	ladder	deceit
bespoke	tired	towering	tall	alert
squirm	loving	category	generous	ambitious
giant	stationary	invigorated	wealthy	valour
short	wriggle	type	sleepy	inconsiderate

i)   Find **three** antonyms for the word 'fatigued'.

_____   _____   _____

ii)   Find **two** synonyms for the word 'writhe'.

_____   _____

iii) Find **two** antonyms for the word 'kind'.

_____   _____

iv)   Find **three** synonyms for the word 'lofty'.

_____   _____   _____

Analogies

Underline the **two** words, **one** from each group, that complete the sentence in the best way.

31. **Clam** is to (broth, overfill, shellfish) as **weasel** is to (stoat, mammal, cunning).

32. **Guest** is to (host, guessed, hotel) as **mews** is to (kitten, entertain, muse).

33. **Reply** is to (respond, rely, telegram) as **skate** is to (board, stroll, sate).

/10

Odd ones out

Underline the **two** words in each group that are different from the other three.

34. boulder   bough   pebble   stone   precipice

35. traditional   irregular   revival   peculiar   abnormal

36. diesel   illness   coal   infection   petrol

Word connections

In the questions below, there are two pairs of words in brackets. Choose from the five possible answers the **one** word that goes equally well with **both** the word pairs. Underline the word.

37. vegetable   squash   crush   orange   juice   (pumpkin, gourd)   (flatten, compress)

38. scheme   window   plot   hatch   arch   (plan, devise)   (opening, door)

Singular and plural

Complete each sentence, using the plural form of the word in brackets.

39. There are four _____ (bus) into town every hour.

40. The mysterious parcel was more than two _____ (foot) wide.

Choose the correct plural to complete the sentence. Underline your answer.

41. There are numerous *possibilities / possabilities / possibilitys* but we must uncover the true cause.

42. His failures outnumbered his *succeses / successes / successers*.

Root words, prefixes and suffixes

Find the roots of these words. Write each answer on the line.

43. enact _____

44. claustrophobia _____

Add the correct prefix or suffix to complete the sentence in the best way.

45. I found his behaviour extremely ___ ___ mature.

46. We visited the museum and _____ (after) made our way to the station.

/13

Word classes

47. Underline the preposition in the sentence below.

The shoes belong to Christine.

48. Complete the table using words from the sentence below.

I rarely looked through the old set of photographs.

Collective noun	Adjective	Adverb	Verb

49. Circle the connective that completes the sentence below in the best way.

Niall smiled at the man   but   /   therefore   /   despite   thinking he was rude.

Word tenses

Rewrite the sentence below using the past tense.

50. Dogs are howling outside.

_____

Write the correct tense of the verb in brackets to complete each sentence.

51. I have been _____ (travel) for six months.

Missing letter

Find the **one** missing letter that will complete both pairs of words. It will end the words before the brackets and start the words after the brackets.

52. tende (____) atio   erro (____) elish

     A. l   **B.** p   **C.** e   **D.** r   **E.** m

53. dau (____) road   bul (____) owl

     A. b   **B.** k   **C.** t   **D.** d   **E.** p

Move a letter

Move **one** letter from the first word to the second word to make **two** new words. Circle the letter.

54. board   note

     A. b   **B.** o   **C.** a   **D.** r   **E.** d

55. quilt   pace

     A. q   **B.** u   **C.** i   **D.** l   **E.** t

Word ladders

Change the first word into the last word. Change only one letter at a time and make **two** new, different words in the middle.

56. MINT   _____   _____   HUNG

57. GROW   _____   _____   BLOT   /11

Missing three letters

The word or letter in capitals has had three letters next to each other taken out. These three letters make one correctly spelt word without changing the order. Write the word on the line.

58. The grey wolf **HED** at the moon.   _____

59. My **GDMA** needs to wear her glasses for reading.   _____

60. I went to the shop and **ST** all my pocket money.   _____

61. For dinner, we had chicken and brown **R**.   _____

Words with letters in common

Underline the only word that **can** be made using the letters of the word on the left.

62. A D V A N C E S   cavern   ascend   caused   canvases   invades

In the group of words below, circle the **two** words that are spelt using the same letters.

63. SORT   TOES   SORE   ROTE   ROSE

Spot the word

Find the hidden four-letter word in each sentence below. Underline the word and write it on the line.

64. Some children think teachers know everything.   _____

65. The views alter depending on the light.   _____

66. My team chose all the best players.   _____

67. Felt tips for sale – five in a packet!   _____

Join two words to make one

Underline the **two** words, **one** from each group, that together make **one** new word. The word from the first group comes first.

68. (with rat moth)   (her our herd)

Find **one** word that can be added to the end of each of the following words to make three new correctly spelt words.

69. import _____   pleas _____   triumph _____

/12

Add or remove a letter to make a new word

Which **one** letter can be added to the beginning of each of the words below to make new words?

70. ilk   aid   urge   harp   ____

Remove **one** letter from the word in capitals to make a new word. The meaning of the new word is given in brackets. Write the word on the line.

71. COURSE (spell)   _____

Spot spelling mistakes

The sentence below contains a word that is spelt incorrectly. Underline the word and write its correct spelling on the line.

72. The ancient house was rumoured to be home to a spector.   _____

Underline the correct spelling of the word that completes the sentence.

73. She did not conferm / confirm / confurm her attendance.

Complete the sentence below by filling in the missing letters.

74. Did he a __ p __ __ c __ a t __ your hard work?

Anagrams

Unjumble the letters of the words in capitals. The words should complete the sentence so that it makes sense. Write your answers on the lines.

75. The TELAFLE _____ that was posted through the door was eye-catchingly

CLUROFOLU _____ .

Unjumble the letters in capitals to make a word. The word is linked to the first two words. Write your answer on the line.

76. knowledgeable   memorised   ELDANRE   _____

Find the letter missing from the muddled word

The sentences below contain two words that have had their letters muddled up. Both words have had the same letter removed from them. Put the letters in order and find the letter that is missing from both. Write your answer on the line.

77. The scientist did not **UTBD** that her **RYHTE** was correct.   ____

78. Once the flowers begin to **ACDE**, you must **PMTE** the vase.   ____

/9

Word grids

Fit these words into the blank spaces in the word grid. Use all of the words. One letter has been placed into the grid to help you.

79. **i)**   anthem   **iii)** llamas   **v)**   domain

  ii) schism   **iv)** lapsed   **vi)** stamen

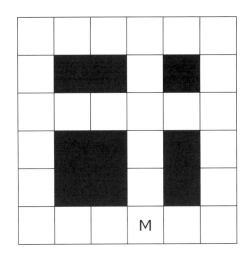

Select words to complete a sentence

From each set of brackets, select the word that completes the sentence below in the best way. Underline your answers.

80. The tourists decided that there was (plenty, little, always) to see in the city, so they went

  (hiking, climb, trudged) in the countryside (although, moreover, instead).

Select the word that completes the sentence below in the best way. Circle your answer. Then write it on the line.

81. My supportive colleagues _____ my petition eagerly.

  A. rejected   **B.** tore   **C.** signed   **D.** chanted   **E.** naming

Homophones

Underline the words that complete the sentence in the best way.

82. The whole class furrowed their *browse / brows* as the teacher wrote the complicated

  sum / some on the *board / bored*.

In the sentence below, underline the **two** homophones that have been used incorrectly.

83. The bawled man was painting the sealing with white paint.

/10

Practice test

Select words to complete a paragraph

84. Using each of the words in the box below once, complete the paragraph by filling in the missing words.

liberty	discontented	day	steady
wanted	years	week	stable

I was quite happy in my new place, and if there was one thing that I missed it must not be

thought I was   **i)**   _____; all who had to do with me were good and I had a

light airy   **ii)**   _____ and the best of food. What more could I want? Why,

liberty! For three years and a half of my life I had had all the   **iii)**   _____

I could wish for; but now, week after   **iv)**   _____, month after month, and

no doubt year after year, I must stand up in a stable night and   **v)**   _____

except when I am   **vi)**   _____, and then I must be just as

vii)   _____ and quiet as any old horse who has worked twenty

viii)   _____.

From Black Beauty by Anna Sewell

Rearrange words to make a sentence

In each sentence below, underline the two words that need to swap places for it to make sense.

85. She sipped the hot carefully coffee.   86. The from stooped to drink giraffe the pool.

Find the superfluous word

For each question below, make a sentence using all but one of the words. Write the sentence on the line and underline the word that you do not use.

87. found it Sophie accept must behaviour no to that difficult she her apologise for

_____

88. door slow the walking trembled I as listened to I the footsteps approaching

_____

/12

Schofield & Sims

Practice test

Complete the word

Add the missing letters to complete the words in the extract below.

89. The **i)** s __ __ __ n t __ s t carefully added the **ii)** p o __ __ e r to the flask and

watched as the **iii)** __ i x __ u __ e began to **iv)** f __ __ m. She had not conducted

this **v)** e __ p __ r __ __ e n t before and she was **vi)** __ __ c i __ e d to see the

vii) r __ __ __ l t s.

In the extract below there are **five** incomplete words. Write the complete words, correctly spelt, on the lines to the right of the box.

90.

The o r __ __ m __ n t fell from the mantelpiece with a t __ __ d, making Mina start. The cat, who had been a __ __ e __ p t __ n g to get Mina's a __ t __ __ __ i o n for some time, f __ __ g __ e d innocence.	**i)** _____ **ii)** _____ **iii)** _____ **iv)** _____ **v)** _____

Number sequences

Find the missing number in the sequence and write it on the line.

91. (_____) 2.5   25   250   2500   25000

92. 200   18   100   (_____)   50   30   25   36

93. 6   9   15   24   39   63   (_____)

Letters for numbers

In these questions, letters stand for numbers. Use the information given to answer the sum. Write your answer as a letter.

94. A = 80   B = 5   C = 37   D = 52   E = 34 $A \div B + (D - E) =$ _____

95. A = 8   B = 25   C = 5   D = 75   E = 585 $B \times A - C \times B =$ _____

Use the set of numbers below to answer the questions that follow.

A = 21, B = 17, C = 28, D = 23, E = 12, F = 19

96. What is the value of the letters in the word BADE? _____

Missing number

Find the missing number in these equations and write it on the line.

97. $60 \times 11 -$ _____ $= 5 \times 2 \times 50 + 75$

98. $35 \div (45 \div 9) = (29 + 27) \div$ _____

/20

Number connections

The number in the square brackets is made using the numbers on either side. Work out the missing number and write it on the line.

99. (27 [45] 9)   (35 [59] 12)   (19 [_____] 23)

100. (100 [12] 2)   (50 [25] 20)   (110 [_____] 8)

Number logic

101. If I add 12 to a third of this number, the answer is half of 90.   _____

102. Adding half of this number to itself makes 30.   _____

Days and dates

103. If 5th December is a Thursday, what day will New Year's Eve fall on?   _____

104. How many Sundays would there be in November if the first of the month is a Friday?   _____

Time

105. Kathleen leaves for work at 09:10, twenty-five minutes after Gregory arrives at work. It takes Paula twice as long to reach work as Jinan. It takes Arjun one hour and ten minutes to get to work. He leaves thirty minutes after Gregory sets off and arrives fifteen minutes after Kathleen arrives. It takes Kathleen forty-five minutes to travel to work. How long is Gregory's journey to work?   _____

106. Antonio's flight leaves London at 18:05. It takes 7 hours and 40 minutes to reach Canada. When he arrives Antonio sets his watch to the time in Canada, which is 5 hours behind England. It then takes him 1 hour and 50 minutes to reach his hotel. According to Antonio's watch, what time is it when he arrives at the hotel?   _____

Position

107. Six friends are different heights. Ayan is taller than James, who is shorter than Zaid and David. David is shorter than Ayan but taller than Zaid. Leo is taller than Zaid but shorter than Neil. Ayan is the third tallest. Who is the shortest?   _____

/9

Sorting information

108. Eloise wears red socks on Tuesdays, Thursdays and Saturdays. She wears blue socks the rest of the week. Gretchen always wears blue socks on Tuesdays and Saturdays and yellow socks on Wednesdays and Sundays. She wears red socks on the days before she wears blue socks and the days after she wears yellow socks. Yetunde alternates red and yellow socks throughout the week, starting with yellow on a Monday. On which day of the week do all three girls wear the same colour socks? _____

109. You can buy a bus ticket with cash or use a card. 16 people board the bus and 9 pay with cash. At the first stop, 7 people leave the bus, 4 of whom had paid by card. Another 8 people get on and half of this group pay with cash. Of the people now on the bus, how many have bought their ticket using a card? _____

True statements

110. If the statements shown in **bold** are true, which **one** of the statements listed beneath them is also true?

A year has 12 months.

There are 52 weeks in a year.

   A.   A year is a long time.

   B.   A year has four seasons.

   C.   Leap years occur every four years.

   D.   It takes the Earth a year to orbit the Sun.

   E.   On average, a month is just over four weeks long.   **Answer:** _____

111. If the statements shown in **bold** are true, which **one** of the statements listed beneath them is **not** true?

Ava and Charlotte have six pet guinea pigs.

Half the guinea pigs are male.

Two of the female guinea pigs are black and white.

Three of the male guinea pigs are ginger.

One of the female guinea pigs is brown.

Only the ginger guinea pigs have rosettes.

   A.   The ginger guinea pigs are all female.

   B.   None of the male guinea pigs are brown.

   C.   The male guinea pigs are larger than the females.

   D.   None of the female guinea pigs have rosettes.

   E.   Guinea pigs eat hay.   **Answer:** _____

/4

Total score:	/142	Time taken:	

Word and letter patterns

Alphabet positions (pages 5–8)

1. n	8. p	15. e
2. u	9. v	16. bead
3. l	10. n	17. decade
4. 26	11. l	18. ebbed
5. 5	12. c	19. l
6. 2	13. s	20. q
7. u	14. o	21. August

Alphabetical order (pages 9–11)

1. i	5. i	9. slake
2. n	6. m	10. motion
3. l	7. having	11. girder
4. g	8. credit	12. unwary

Letter sequences (pages 12–14)

1. **OZ** (+1 = O, +2 = Z)
2. **BT** (−3 = B, +3 = T)
3. **UF** (−1 = U, +1 = F)
4. **PA** (+2 = P, −1 = A)
5. **XZ** (+3 +1 +3 +1 +3 = XZ)
6. **IJ** (+5 +4 +3 +2 +1 = IJ)
7. **II** (−2 −1 −2 −1 −2 = I, −1 −2 −1 −2 −1 = I)
8. **SY** (−1 −2 −3 −4 −5 = S, +1 +2 +3 +4 +5 = Y)

These are all **leapfrogging sequences:**

9. **AC** SU **DF** VX **GI** YA = **JL** (+3)
10. **PO** DC **ML** BA **JI** ZY = **GF** (−3)
11. **RO** FD **SP** GE **UR** IG **XU** LJ = **BY** (+1 +2 +3 +4)
12. **PT** DC **OS** FE **LP** GF **KO** IH = **HL** (−1 −3 −1 −3)
13. **CS** (−3 = C, −1 = S)
14. **SQ** (+1 = S, +1 = Q)
15. **US** (−5 = U, −5 = S – sequence +5 +4 +3 +2)
16. **FB** (+2 = F, −5 = B)
17. **MW** (+2 = M, +2 = W – alternating gap of +2 +1)
18. **UJ** (+4 = U, +4 = J – sequence +5 +4 +3 +2)
19. **LH** (−2 = L, +2 = H – sequence −1 −2 −3 −4 for first letter, +1 +2 +3 +4 for second letter)
20. **SQ** (+2 = S, +2 = Q – sequence +1 +2 +3 +4)

Letter codes (pages 15–17)

1. **Y** (both numbered 2)	15. **KO** (numbered 11 12)
2. **O** (both numbered 12)	16. **AF** (numbered 1 6)
3. **T** (both numbered 7)	17. **IW** (numbered 9 4)
4. **F** (both numbered 6)	18. **OP** (numbered 12 11)
5. **L** (both numbered 12)	19. **OG** (numbered 12 7)
6. **H** (both numbered 8)	20. **BT** (numbered 2 7)
7. **R** (both numbered 9)	21. **GI** (+3 +3)
8. **C** (both numbered 3)	22. **NQ** (−2 −2)
9. **V** (both numbered 5)	23. **MH** (+3 −2)
10. **D** (both numbered 4)	24. **IL** (+5 +4)
11. **M** (both numbered 13)	25. **OR** (−8 −8)
12. **P** (both numbered 11)	26. **TH** (+5 −5)
13. **IH** (numbered 9 8)	27. **VH** (+8 −2)
14. **EC** (numbered 5 3)	28. **MD** (−3 +4)

Word codes (pages 18–21)

1. **XLDH**	5. **ZMTIB**	9. **DREAM**
2. **HRMT**	6. **RMHVXG**	10. **GIRAFFE**
3. **XLZXS**	7. **YARD**	11. **PLANE**
4. **KLMB**	8. **DARK**	12. **ABOUT**

13. **HSFFO** (+1 +1 +1 +1 +1)
14. **PTHDS** (−1 −1 −1 −1 −1)
15. **UTHI** (+1 +2 +3 +4)
16. **EAZOS** (−1 −4 −1 −4 −1)
17. **VBLDQBH** (+3 −1 +3 −1 +3 −1 +3)
18. **YMZXP** (+5 −5 +5 −5 +5)
19. **BUSH** (−1 −1 −1 −1)
20. **GULL** (+2 −2 +2 −2)
21. **LAUGHTER** (−2 +1 −2 +1 −2 +1 −2 +1)
22. **^ ! " $**   23. **TENT**   24. **APE**

Match the codes (page 23)

1.
3497	8467	3495	8497
SHIP	CHOP	SHIN	CHIP

   i) 3467   **ii) 79584**

2.
3419	9841	9517	3519
SING	GAIN	GONE	SONG

   i) 3551   **ii) 89841**

3.
1234	4521	4362	1732
TRAP	PORT	PAIR	TEAR

   i) PART   **ii) 172252**

Schofield & Sims

Answers

Make a word from one other word
(pages 24–26)

1. (pant pan) (band ban) (seem **see**)
   (remove last letter)

2. (tram ram) (twin win) (boat **oat**)
   (remove first letter)

3. (hop shop) (aid said) (ash **sash**)
   (add **s** to the beginning)

4. (many man) (seed see) (lady **lad**)
   (remove last letter)

5. (all ball) (ore pore) (ear **fear**)
   (add to the beginning of the word the letter that comes next in the alphabet after the first letter of the word; for example, in (**all ball**) the first letter is **a** and the next letter in the alphabet after **a** is **b** – add **b** to **all** to make **ball**)

6. (grown gown) (steal seal) (black **back**)
   (remove second letter)

7. (table tale) (tire tie) (bleed **bled**)
   (remove third letter)

8. (grain rain) (tread read) (cloud **loud**)
   (remove first letter)

9. (bend bed) (sand sad) (burn **bun**)
   (remove third letter)

10. (tramp trap) (grind grid) (beard **bead**)
    (remove fourth letter)

11. (party trap) (stare rats) (liver **evil**)

12. (tinsel lint) (leaded deal) (denies **send**)

13. (amused muse) (staked take) (phoned **hone**)

14. (crawls law) (growls low) (tootle **lot**)

15. (please slap) (treads drat) (brought **grub**)

16. (around ran) (apart pat) (abound **ban**)

17. (trail rat) (though hot) (troop **rot**)

18. (ground rod) (spoilt pot) (stolen **ton**)

19. (ambush ham) (inward din) (aghast **tag**)

20. (adrift rift) (entail tail) (appear **pear**)

21. (bellow low) (maggot got) (barrow **row**)

22. (juggle leg) (muddle led) (window **own**)

23. (proper pope) (weaker wake) (fronds **fond**)

24. (stones nest) (stewed west) (deacon **code**)

25. (dribble bile) (bramble bale) (whistle **tile**)

26. (asleep pale) (haunts shun) (instil **list**)

27. (bottle lot) (middle lid) (toggle **log**)

28. (doted dot) (metal let) (timed **dim**)

29. (dented dent) (forest tore) (lunged **dung**)

30. (denote teen) (handle lean) (galore **real**)

Make a word from two other words
(pages 27–28)

1. (help [hear] pair) (soup [**sort**] grit)

2. (night [this] sulk) (cream [**mare**] entry)

3. (magic [aged] mode) (lever [**even**] line)

4. (shop [save] vane) (pace [**plan**] alone)

5. (sound [done] lake) (peels [**self**] leaf)

6. (shower [wash] army) (thumb [**moth**] open)

7. (hand [hint] site) (lash [**lost**] moth)

8. (drop [dear] vase) (clap [**coal**] halo)

9. (melt [test] spot) (leap [**perk**] rink)

10. (drop [rope] plea) (them [**heat**] arts)

11. (rush [husk] risk) (leer [**rein**] pain)

12. (need [dens] soup) (nets [**sent**] time)

13. (rattle [right] sigh) (hanger [**heron**] hero)

14. (balloon [lands] skid) (hobbles [**bossy**] yams)

15. (spring [sworn] crown) (fright [**flail**] small)

16. (clamour [acorn] crones) (trundle [**under**] nearly)

Word and letter patterns practice page 1 (page 29)

1. d	6. deface	11. g
2. 15	7. ceded	12. crowd
3. q	8. Monday	13. weight
4. i	9. l	14. corrupt
5. l	10. i	

Word and letter patterns practice page 2 (page 30)

1. **VU** (+2 = V, +2 = U)

2. **QJ** (−1 = Q, +1 = J)

3. **CD** (leapfrogging: +2 = C, +2 = D)

4. **PX** (−3 = P, +3 = X)

5. **FI** (−4 = F, +4 = I)

6. **UC** (−7 = U, +7 = C)

7. **KM** (+3, +3)

8. **KN** (letter partners numbered 11, 13)

9. **VU** (letter partners numbered 5, 6)

10. **TW** (+2, +2)

11. **ZU** (+3, −1)

12. **OK** (letter partners numbered 12, 11)

13. **QSCOIF** (+2 +1 +2 +1 +2 +1)

14. **JMHFGS** (−1 −1 −1 −1 −1 −1)

Answers

Word and letter patterns practice

page 2 (page 30) continued

15. DRIZZLE (letter partners 4, 9, 9, 1, 1, 12, 5)

16. LEMON (−1 −2 −3 −4 −5)

17. + ☼ ♦♦ & ⌂

18.
| 3451 | 3463 | 1487 | 7463 |
| THIS | THAT | SHOW | WHAT |

i) 3451   **ii) 3467**   **iii) WASH**

19.
| 6891 | 9136 | 7839 | 6873 |
| MOST | STEM | DOES | MODE |

i) 9136   **ii) 68879**   **iii) SEEDS**

Word and letter patterns practice

page 3 (page 31)

1. (west wet) (best bet) (fast **fat**)

2. (chain chin) (grain grin) (breed **bred**)

3. (waddle lad) (little lit) (meddle **led**)

4. (matron tram) (poster stop) (masher **sham**)

5. (rampart ramp) (lantern rant) (mentors **rent**)

6. (assures sure) (redeems seem) (staring **grin**)

7. (shut hut) (bran ran) (grub **rub**)

8. (bush bus) (song son) (team **tea**)

9. (rotten not) (mitten nit) (logged **dog**)

10. (feast seat) (clasp slap) (hints **tins**)

11. (weed [tore] root) (pies [late] tall)

12. (white [with] trawl) (height [nice] crane)

13. (wand [dawn] dear) (bust [tubs] tent)

14. (bangs [bond] bound) (stale [lies] lines)

15. (flower [slow] houses) (thanks [than] hostels)

16. (windows [chins] coaches) (barrage [spare] whisper)

17. (weep [pray] tray) (door [ring] sing)

18. (table [grab] green) (misty [this] there)

19. (fancy [funny] haiku) (burly [berry] prime)

20. (vines [invest] nest) (ashen [shawls] owls)

Vocabulary

Word meanings (page 33)

1. **B** (useless)   **3.** **C** (regret)

2. **D** (referred)   **4.** **A** (accept)

Sort words into groups (pages 34–35)

1. **i)** **C** (type of nut)   **iv)** **B** (type of metal)

ii) **A** (type of mammal)   **v)** **D** (type of insect)

iii) **D** (type of insect)   **vi)** **C** (type of nut)

2. **A constellation** (formations of stars)

3. **D sabre** (types of sword)

4.

Abstract nouns	Beverages	Modes of transport
confusion	cider	toboggan
charity	soda	rickshaw
pleasure	cordial	glider

Ordering words (page 36)

1. pond (physical size: **droplet, puddle, pond, lake, ocean**)

2. parallelogram (number of sides: **circle, triangle, parallelogram, pentagon, hexagon**)

3. interested (intensity of emotion: **bored, ambivalent, interested, fascinated, obsessed**)

4. city (physical size: **village, town, city, country, continent**)

5. gram (physical size: **milligram, centigram, gram, kilogram, tonne**)

6. starling (physical size: **midge, gerbil, starling, vulture, rhinoceros**)

Synonyms (pages 37–40)

1. (**almost** always never) (sometimes **nearly** now)

2. (repeat **reply** redo) (undo **answer** refuse)

3. (sturdy detail **fragile**) (**delicate** broken grand)

4. (**essential** essence easy) (hard **important** difficult)

5. (**diminish** dessert disaster) (leave **reduce** increase)

6. (strong **weak** week) (small **frail** month)

7. (sweet **sour** batter) (**bitter** lemon arrive)

8. (free **compliment** complex) (**flatter** argue ignore)

9. **ask** talk reply annoy **question**

10. blame **defeat** assure **beat** lose

11. hound feline artistic **sneaky crafty**

12. **destiny** detour aloud **fate** fete

13. class firm soft **busy engaged**

14. intent **impolite** distress **rude** polite

15. **bicycle** runway station **bus** wing

16. lamp **kitchen** shed carpet **bedroom**

17. sneak   **23.** drink

18. careful   **24.** flee

19. outcome   **25.** find

20. positive, certain   **26.** friendly

21. tremble, shake   **27.** thoughtful

22. criticise, denounce   **28.** expensive

Answers

Antonyms (pages 41–44)

1. (**begin** after stop) (lend land **end**)
2. (danger **despair** desperate) (risk **hope** fear)
3. (**mean** dark poor) (dim dreary **kind**)
4. (find **full** fast) (**empty** quick found)
5. (healthy **include** inside) (hungry interior **exclude**)
6. (movie **genuine** genius) (real **fake** film)
7. (perfect pendant **new**) (brand **antique** perform)
8. (**accept** letter gift) (receive thank **reject**)
9. divulge, conceal
10. maximum, minimum
11. powerful, feeble
12. stretch, compress
13. ignorance
14. help
15. discourage
16. indifferent
17. straight
18. loss
19. fool
20. rare
21. modest
22. destroy
23. interesting
24. automated

Synonym and antonym grids (page 45)

1. i)   pending, unsettled, outstanding
    ii) split, separate
    iii) false, contrived
    iv) contaminate, corrupt, pollute

Analogies (pages 46–48)

1. Fish is to (walk, run, **swim**) as bird is to (trot, **fly**, jump).
2. Grass is to (long, **green**, mow) as sand is to (warm, beach, **yellow**).
3. Uncle is to (old, son, **aunt**) as sister is to (mother, girl, **brother**).
4. Eleven is to (**twelve**, number, two) as four is to (seven, for, **five**).
5. Teacher is to (bank, park, **school**) as mechanic is to (car, **garage**, tip).
6. Elephant is to (large, **hide**, trunk) as dog is to (seek, tail, **coat**).
7. Left is to (leave, **right**, wrong) as horizontal is to (sun, across, **vertical**).
8. Attack is to (fight, win, **defend**) as expand is to (extinct, **contract**, explain).
9. Fresh is to (**stale**, edible, air) as humble is to (old, pie, **proud**).
10. Rush is to (**dawdle**, jog, skip) as adequate is to (**inadequate**, less, quad).
11. Clear is to (wash, **cloudy**, simple) as late is to (eight, cup, **early**).

12. Reward is to (**penalty**, restore, revoke) as relevant is to (expect, recent, **meaningless**).
13. Main is to (horse, **mane**, least) as sight is to (picture, taste, **site**).
14. Gardener is to (plants, grow, **spade**) as painter is to (artist, **brush**, colour).
15. Stag is to (deer, doe, **antlers**) as bull is to (**horns**, calf, field).
16. Taps is to (tops, money, **spat**) as dab is to (dot, **bad**, dip).
17. Tree is to (trunk, twigs, **roots**) as building is to (flat, **foundations**, home).
18. Challenge is to (succeed, finish, **dare**) as implore is to (improve, endure, **beseech**).

Odd ones out (page 49)

1. **mosquito, cricket** (the others are all flowers)
2. **organ, guitar** (the others are all types of jobs)
3. **delight, joy** (the others are sad emotions)
4. **yacht, canoe** (the others are all types of air transport)
5. **owl, kestrel** (the others are all mammals)
6. **lettuce, salad** (the others are all types of fruit)
7. **obedience, faith** (the others are all synonyms)
8. **first, gram** (the others are all measures of time)

Word connections (page 50)

1. **row** (the word rhyming with **toe** goes with [paddle, propel] and the word rhyming with **cow** goes with [fight, argue])
2. **tear** (the word rhyming with **air** goes with [rip, cut] and the word rhyming with **ear** goes with [cry, weep])
3. **wound** (the word with long **oo** sound goes with [injury, hurt] and the word rhyming with **sound** goes with [turned, twisted])
4. **invalid** (the word with stress on **in**valid goes with [patient, injured] and the word with stress on in**val**id goes with [defunct, obsolete])
5. **close** (the word rhyming with **nose** goes with [shut, cover] and the word rhyming with **dose** goes with [near, almost])
6. **sow** (the word rhyming with **so** goes with [plant, cultivate] and the word rhyming with **cow** goes with [pig, hog])
7. **band** (the two words 'band' are **homonyms**. They mean: 'a strip of colour' and 'a set of people')
8. **date** (the two homonyms mean: 'a type of fruit' and 'a meeting with another person')

Answers

Vocabulary practice page 1 (page 51)

1. **A** (determination)
2. **E** (luxurious)
3. **B** (applicant)
4. **E** (personality)
5. **C** (disease)
6. **D** (skeletal)

Vocabulary practice page 2 (page 52)

1. i)   **D** (3D shape)
    ii) **B** (shade of white)
    iii) **A** (type of spice)
    iv) **C** (animal with four legs)
    v)   **B** (shade of white)
    vi) **D** (3D shape)

2. i)   **C** (synonyms of 'upset')
    ii) **A** (dimensions)
    iii) **D** (cooking methods)
    iv) **D** (cooking methods)
    v)   **B** (plants with thorns/prickles)
    vi) **C** (synonyms of 'upset')

3. **B debate** (synonyms of 'conversation')

4. **C might** (modal verbs)

5.

Clothing	Writing systems	Punctuation marks
leotard	runes	hyphen
sarong	braille	colon
dungarees	hieroglyphs	ellipsis

Vocabulary practice page 3 (page 53)

1. **angry** (intensity of emotion: **tranquil, irked, angry, enraged, incandescent**)

2. **satsuma** (physical size: **blueberry, strawberry, satsuma, artichoke, watermelon**)

3. **motorbike** (number of wheels: **ski, unicycle, motorbike, tricycle, lorry**)

4. **decade** (length of time: **moment, fortnight, decade, lifetime, eon**)

5. **sunflower** (height of mature plant: **moss, dandelion, sunflower, oak, redwood**)

6. **gust** (strength: **calm, breeze, gust, gale, hurricane**)

7. (bargain question **baffle**) (**confuse** price answer)

8. (thankful **bold** afraid) (bald **fearless** praise)

9. dull **racket** sport **din** shiny

10. **conflict** peace part **feud** avoid

11. **tranquil**

12. **surpass**

13. **ask, request**

14. **erase, delete**

15. **fight**
16. **try**
17. **container**
18. **valiant**

Vocabulary practice page 4 (page 54)

1. (new **ancient** ancestor) (**modern** moderate moreover)

2. (**artificial** arrange entrance) (fake **natural** unkind)

3. **optimist, pessimist**

4. **complex, simple**

5. **tidy**

6. **strict**

7. **confident**

8. i)   **insignificant, unimportant, petty**
    ii) **precise, clear**
    iii) **rotten, decayed**
    iv) **stable, serene, tranquil**

Vocabulary practice page 5 (page 55)

1. Over is to (down, **under**, out) as enter is to (entrance, into, **exit**).

2. Racket is to (noise, **badminton**, cricket) as stick is to (tree, **hockey**, glue).

3. Ball is to (cry, **bawl**, bowl) as seam is to (seal, dress, **seem**).

4. Fashion is to (clothes, **trend**, model) as bet is to (**wager**, bat, win).

5. Clarinet is to (music, **wind**, play) as drum is to (**percussion**, sticks, loud).

6. Apple is to (fruit, red, **pip**) as plum is to (vegetable, juicy, **stone**).

7. Leap is to (**pale**, jump, high) as rear is to (**rare**, rhyme, steer).

8. Hire is to (**recruit**, lower, high) as ability is to (clever, **aptitude**, agility).

9. **acorn, flower** (the others are types of tree)

10. **church, temple** (the others are educational buildings)

11. **fear, delight** (the others are anger words)

12. **increase, inflate** (the others all mean to get smaller)

13. **doctor, nurse** (the others are different words for young people)

14. **sleep, dream** (the others are things you sleep in)

15. **seal, dolphin** (the others are all fish)

16. **brother, uncle** (the others are all female)

17. **change** (the two homonyms mean: 'coins, or money you get back when you pay with more than what is needed' and 'to start being different')

Schofield & Sims

Answers

18. **wind** (the word rhyming with **sinned** goes with [gale, breeze] and the word rhyming with **mind** goes with [turn, rotate])

19. **subject** (the word with the stress on **sub**ject goes with [topic, lesson] and the word with the stress on sub**ject** goes with [inflict, expose])

20. **sewer** (the word rhyming with **newer** goes with [drain, effluent] and the word rhyming with **lower** goes with [seamstress, tailor])

21. **wave** (the two homonyms mean: 'a moving line on the surface of water' and 'a hand gesture that you use to greet a friend')

22. **star** (the two homonyms mean: 'a bright object seen in the sky at night' and 'a very famous person')

23. **case** (the two homonyms mean: 'an incident that is investigated by lawyers' and 'a box to keep or carry things in')

24. **land** (the two homonyms mean: 'to come back to the land after being on a plane or a ship' and 'the part of the Earth not covered by sea')

Grammar

Singular and plural (page 56)

1. thieves
2. discoveries
3. videos
4. cacti/cactuses
5. werewolves
6. beliefs
7. crises
8. dominoes
9. peaches
10. loyalties

Root words, prefixes and suffixes (page 57)

1. pure
2. respect
3. lead
4. mis (misfortune)
5. hungriest
6. preheat

Word classes (page 59)

1. The teacher congratulated **me** for winning the prize.

2.

Adjective	loudest	tuneful
Adverb	definitely	least
Verb	is	thought
Common noun	singer	choir
Proper noun	Jenny	Annabel

3. After I have finished **eating** this piece of cherry cake, I will wash my hands.

4. driven
5. otherwise
6. except

Word tenses (page 60)

1. Anisa drew in her sketchbook.
2. The student spoke to the professor.
3. He ran an errand for his parents and then did his homework.
4. hoping
5. could
6. beaten

Grammar practice page 1 (page 61)

1. scratches
2. dictionaries
3. tomatoes
4. runners-up
5. cherries
6. deer
7. shelves
8. salmon
9. memories
10. loaves
11. bicycles
12. roofs
13. kind
14. need
15. mature
16. norm/normal
17. comfort
18. cycle
19. ful (thankful)
20. disobey
21. disadvantage
22. hopeful
23. politely
24. loneliness

Grammar practice page 2 (page 62)

1. It was raining heavily **but** we had to give the dogs a walk.

2.

Adjective	determined	groundbreaking
Adverb	recently	carefully
Verb	landed	built
Common noun	scientists	robot
Proper noun	Mars	America

3. Her colleague went ahead without waiting for her to make the decision.

4. brought
5. before
6. My sister went to the theatre to watch a ballet performance.
7. I took my dog for a walk.
8. dreamt/dreamed
9. beginning
10. preparing

Spelling

Missing letter (pages 63–64)

1. **e** (spine, eyes)
2. **m** (stream, meat)
3. **t** (greet, tomb)
4. **p** (soup, piglet)
5. **n** (town, neck)
6. **a** (sofa, apple)
7. **k** (walk, king, milk, kite)
8. **p** (clap, pine, leap, pound)
9. **e** (wave, eat, time, earth)
10. **g** (sting, gnat, drag, glare)
11. **n** (train, nought, grin, near)
12. **l** (mill, lake, steal, live)
13. **st** (waist, stand)
14. **ce** (bounce, ceiling)
15. **us** (virus, usage)
16. **le** (tremble, learn)
17. **sp** (grasp, spend)
18. **or** (major, organ)

Move a letter (page 65)

1. **n (year, snail)**
2. **r (bought, drown)**
3. **c (lamp, chill)**
4. **t (rust, burnt)**
5. **r (band, heard)**
6. **g (rain, began)**

Word ladders (pages 66–67)

1. **BEND**
2. **LOSS**
3. **POUR**
4. **TOAD**
5. **VOLE**
6. **HEAP**
7. **HAIL, HALL**
8. **PURE, SURE**
9. **BALE, MALE**
10. **GUST, DUST**
11. **PICK, PACK**
12. **FILE, PILE**

Missing three letters (pages 68–69)

1. **HAT** (that) or **HIS** (this)
2. **SIT** (visit)
3. **LIP** (slipped)
4. **ANT** (wants)
5. **HEN** (when)
6. **ust** (illustrate)   **omm** (recommend)
7. **usu** (unusual)   **ter** (entertain)
8. **ell** (rebellion)   **dib** (incredible)

9. **ugh** (thoughtful)   **ide** (considerate)
10. **pec** (unexpected)   **cas** (occasional)
11. **PIT** (hospital)
12. **ARM** (alarmed)
13. **WIT** (switch)

*Check that you have used **horizontal** lines to mark your answers as shown below.*

11.		**12.**		**13.**	
PUT	☐	DOG	☐	WIT	▬
MOP	☐	ARM	▬	RIP	☐
ARE	☐	ROW	☐	CAT	☐
LEG	☐	PEN	☐	DIG	☐
PIT	▬	SUN	☐	LOW	☐

Words with letters in common (page 71)

1. **lunge**
2. **dames**
3. **engine**
4. **topped**
5. **friend**
6. **shouts**
7. **dab, bad**
8. **lacy, clay**

Spot the word (page 72)

1. Have you seen the**m eat** their meal yet? (**meat**)
2. My uncle had hi**s own** aeroplane. (**sown**)
3. You need a war**m ove**n for baking bread. (**move**)
4. The dreadful storm was a weat**her d**isaster. (**herd**)
5. I want to jo**g one** mile each day. (**gone**)
6. Nervously, the competitor**s ent**ered the ring. (**sent**)
7. Kimberly scored **the m**ost points in the test. (**them**)
8. He was the fir**st op**ponent to cross the line. (**stop**)
9. There was a sud**den t**hunder crash. (**dent**)
10. New employees bring ne**w ide**as. (**wide**)

Join two words to make one (pages 73–75)

1. (can **key** car) (band **board** bored) (keyboard)
2. (**puff** poor peer) (on **in** out) (puffin)
3. (by but **be**) (**hind** hound hand) (behind)
4. (**end** and under) (**less** loss lass) (endless)
5. (about **over** even) (near give **take**) (overtake)
6. (paint path **pass**) (**port** part pant) (passport)
7. (leg foot **arm**) (your **our** their) (armour)
8. (try **in** rest) (**quest** round down) (inquest)
9. (see look **hear**) (twenty five **ten**) (hearten)
10. (**sign** train grow) (ape **post** aim) (signpost)

Answers

11. (tar **bar** car) (grin **gain** ten) (bargain)
12. (**post** most pine) (**age** and or) (postage)
13. (is us **as**) (queen **king** prince) (asking)
14. (yes **not** all) (is in **ice**) (notice)
15. (up **so** it) (**lid** led lad) (solid)
16. (**he** him her) (row air **art**) (heart)
17. (miss **to** let) (**wards** take end) (towards)
18. (blue pink **red**) (ant **one** win) (redone)
19. (tear **bar** out) (round key **row**) (barrow)
20. (and out **so**) (at **on** off) (soon)
21. **day** (daytime, daylight, daydream, daybreak)
22. **water** (waterfall, waterfront, waterbed, waterwheel)
23. **sea** (seashell, seashore, seaweed, seasick)
24. **sun** (sunset, sunshine, sundown, suntan)
25. **back** (backpack, backwards, backhand, background)
26. **way** (subway, hallway, midway)
27. **out** (workout, fallout, without)
28. **drop** (eavesdrop, dewdrop, teardrop)
29. **print** (blueprint, footprint, fingerprint)
30. **side** (fireside, downside, lakeside)

Add or remove a letter to make a new word (pages 76–77)

1. d (drifts, drake, delude, damp)
2. h (hours, hairy, hover, hill)
3. t (troll, tweak, twitch, table)
4. o (olive, omen, ozone, opens)
5. a (again, apart, atop, awry)
6. c (clock, cream, clamp, cold)
7. b (blight, brook, beat, bend)
8. s (shoot, stale, shock, sliver)
9. seed (remove w)   13. bushes (add h)
10. fends (remove i)   14. dozen (add n)
11. cram (remove e)   15. ditch (add d)
12. rant (remove g)   16. louse (add u)

Spot spelling mistakes (page 78)

1. enrol   4. hymn
2. surprise   5. receipt
3. musical   6. shielded

Anagrams (pages 79–80)

1. RESPOND   3. CHICKEN, ROOSTER
2. SYRUPY   4. AUDIENCE, ORCHESTRA

5. PAINTING, ANTIQUE   9. FLOURISH
6. CHOIR, THEATRE   10. CRICKET
7. REVEAL   11. PERCH
8. BARGAIN   12. WOUND

Find the letter missing from the muddled word (page 81)

1. i (I put the lollipop STICK into the black RUBBISH bag.)
2. a (The van's BRAKES were so SQUEAKY that they sounded like mice.)
3. t (We bought our pet RABBIT a new HUTCH.)
4. r (The TURKEY squawked excitedly as it pecked at the GRAIN.)
5. g (We had THOUGHT that we would see a GIRAFFE at the zoo.)
6. e (He is going to the THEATRE this EVENING to see a play.)

Word grids (page 84)

1.

H	I	G	H	E	R
A	■	■	E	■	E
L	■	■	R	■	A
O	X	T	A	I	L
E	■	■	L	■	L
D	E	A	D	L	Y

2.

B	E	A	M	E	D
O	■	T	■	■	R
U	P	T	A	K	E
G	■	A	■	■	A
H	■	C	■	■	M
T	O	K	E	N	S

or

B	O	U	G	H	T
E	■	P	■	■	O
A	T	T	A	C	K
M	■	A	■	■	E
E	■	K	■	■	N
D	R	E	A	M	S

Answers

Word grids (page 84) continued

3.

I	T	S
C	A	P
E	R	A

4.

T	W	O
H	E	R
E	B	B

Spelling practice page 1 (page 85)

1. **y** (army, your, play, yacht)
2. **g** (clog, goal, hang, give)
3. **e** (mate, easy, wine, even)
4. **th** (earth, thread)
5. **dy** (sandy, dynamic)
6. **en** (golden, ough)
7. **e (what, weed)**
8. **s (have, barns)**
9. **e (cram, tripe)**
10. **i (nave, lied)**
11. **l (peat, model)**
12. **u (cold, bound)**
13. **FRIED**
14. **MOUND**
15. **CLINK**
16. **SCARS, SCANS**
17. **WAFER, SAFER**
18. **BRAIN, BRAID**

Spelling practice page 2 (page 86)

1. **MAN** (manage)
2. **LID** (slide)
3. **SAY** (essay)
4. **PIN** (spinning)
5. **throne**
6. **dryer**
7. **girth, right**
8. **shale, leash**
9. She smiled **her b**rightest smile. (**herb**)
10. Laug**h and** smile every day! (**hand**)
11. **He ar**rived late and Mum was cross. (**hear**)
12. It's important not to was**te a m**inute! (**team**)
13. (up **count** sing) (out **down** in) (countdown)
14. (**round** under through) (above below **about**) (roundabout)
15. **out** (outdoors, outlive, outpouring, outstation)
16. **as** (asking, assure, ascertain, ascent)

Spelling practice page 3 (page 87)

1. **c** (chip, cover, close, care)
2. **pint** (remove r)
3. **bridge** (add g)
4. **loosely**
5. **difference**
6. **mischief**
7. **ARGUMENT**
8. **CELEBRATE, RESTAURANT**
9. **TREBLE**
10. **HOARSE**
11. **COAST**

Spelling practice page 4 (page 88)

1. **p** (SUPPER was a slice of birthday cake left over from the PARTY.)
2. **d** (Alexa TEASED her brother until her mother SHOUTED at her to stop.)
3. **o** (The elderly woman SPOKE so SOFTLY that it was difficult to hear what she was saying.)

4.

A		F		C
F	O	U	R	T	H
L		U		A
A	P	H	I	D	S
M		T		T
E	N	Z	Y	M	E

5.

A	I	R
G	N	U
E	K	E

Cloze

Select words to complete a sentence (page 91)

1. The (boy, horses, **children**) laughed as they (**teased**, threw, play) each other on their way (underground, **home**, tomorrow).
2. Recorders are my favourite type of (**instrument**, technology, utensil) because they make a (harsher, enjoyment, **gentle**) sound which I (appreciative, **adore**, loathe).
3. **C** (The restaurant received **numerous** complaints about its inhospitable staff.)
4. **E** (She proceeded **cautiously** as she was frightened of losing her way.)
5. It was so dark in the pitch-black cave that Lilian could barely **taste** anything. **see**
6. I **saw** my favourite song playing on the radio. **heard**
7. The grateful king **punished** the brave knight for his courage. **rewarded** (or similar, e.g. thanked, praised)
8. Fictional stories are always (long, exciting, **imaginary**, enjoyable, interesting).
9. Bungalows are never built with (**stairs**, windows, a door, a roof, a conservatory).
10. All doctors are highly (friendly, exhausting, judgemental, sympathetic, **trained**).

Schofield & Sims

Answers

Homophones (page 92)

1. **buy, wait**

2. **route, their**

3. **wrap, allowed**

4. Grandmother was making **doe** in the kitchen. I watched as she **needed** it carefully, wrinkling her nose as flour billowed up from the table. The **cent** of baking filled the air and I **side** happily. I had **mist** her terribly while she had been gone.

5. The **kernel** examined the soldiers closely. She was known **four** punishing **troupes** for **miner** mistakes. However, she had earned their **trussed** as a strong leader.

6. As his father's sole **air**, Jacob inherited the entire fortune. He was especially pleased to receive a beautiful **peace** of jewellery. It was a silver **broach** decorated with **pail** gemstones and **purls**.

Select words to complete a paragraph (page 94)

1. At its most powerful, the Roman Empire **reigned** over more than 45 million people and encompassed **territories** across Europe, North Africa and Asia. As the empire **expanded**, so too did its **centre**, Rome, which grew from a town to a large, bustling city. Rome was home to over one million subjects. Although it is now celebrated for its beautiful **architecture** and **advanced** technology, its vast **population** meant that the city was also a hazardous, **unhygienic** place to live.

2. The new boy went off brushing the dust from his clothes, **sobbing**, snuffling, and **occasionally** looking back and shaking his head and threatening what he would do to Tom the "next time he caught him out." To which Tom responded with **jeers**, and started off in high feather, and as soon as his back was turned the new boy **snatched** up a stone, threw it and hit him between the shoulders and then turned tail and ran like an **antelope**. Tom chased the traitor home, and thus found out where he lived. He then held a position at the gate for some time, **daring** the enemy to come outside, but the enemy only made faces at him through the window and **declined**. At last the enemy's mother appeared, and called Tom a bad, vicious, vulgar child, and **ordered** him away.

Rearrange words to make a sentence (page 95)

1. The farmer **dozen** a **counted** eggs.
   The farmer counted a dozen eggs.

2. The land is difficult **without** navigate **to** a map.
   The land is difficult to navigate without a map.

3. **Green** trees' leaves turned from **the** to yellow.
   The trees' leaves turned from green to yellow.

4. She **every** in her diary **wrote** day.
   She wrote in her diary every day.

5. Organising the festival **weeks** several **took**.
   Organising the festival took several weeks.

6. The beautiful **water** glided through the murky **swan**.
   The beautiful swan glided through the murky water.

7. There **during** a short interval **was** the performance.
   There was a short interval during the performance.

8. He grimaced **stable** he cleaned out the **as**.
   He grimaced as he cleaned out the stable.

9. The **was** display **firework** spectacular.
   The firework display was spectacular.

10. **His** regretted **he** decision immediately.
    He regretted his decision immediately.

Find the superfluous word (page 96)

1. **detention**
   The pupil's poor behaviour did not impress the teacher.

2. **silence**
   A noisy environment can make it difficult to concentrate.

3. **cinema**
   The actor bowed as the audience applauded deafeningly.

4. **it**
   Fortunately the ship was still moored in the harbour.

Complete the word (page 98)

1. The door was locked and although he r **a** t **t** l e d the handle vigorously, Romit could not **f** o r c e it open. He k n **e** l t down and peeked c u r **i** **o** u s l y through the keyhole. The room on the other side of the door was dark and it took his eyes a moment to a **d** j u **s** t. Slowly, he b **e** g **a** n to make out ominous black shapes crouched in the **s** h **a** d **o** w s.

2. As the waves crashed around the little boat, the c **a** p t **a** i n gripped the ship's wheel so t **i** g h t **l** y his k n **u** c **k** l e s turned white. He desperately wanted his c r **e** w to r **e** t r **e** a t below deck but they **r** e **f** **u** s e d to l e **a** v e his side.

3. i) **majestic**   iv) **talons**
   ii) **above**   v) **snatch**
   iii) **hunting**

4. i) **favourite**   iv) **juicy**
   ii) **prepare**   v) **effort**
   iii) **delicious**

Answers

Cloze practice page 1 (page 99)

1. Dhrooti's (**ambition**, fear, imagination) was to (discover, invent, **become**) a scientist so she studied (**constantly**, occasionally, infrequently).

2. The (music, **audience**, moment) fell silent as the (clumsy, tuneful, **elegant**) dancers sprang onto the (**stage**, balcony, programme).

3. **C** (Gleaming gold shone from **beneath** the sleeping dragon's belly.)

4. **D** (Although he had been **reluctant** to go to the party, he very much enjoyed it.)

5. The tree's **roots** moved gently in the wind. **leaves** (or similar, e.g. branches)

6. The teacher **punished** the students for their neat work and tidy desks. **praised** (or similar, e.g. rewarded)

7. Humans need (milk, **oxygen**, limbs, friends, comfort) to survive.

8. All swans are (white, aggressive, dangerous, female, **waterfowl**).

9. **stationery, blue**

10. **to, pier**

11. **road, past**

12. The archaeologist had discovered an ancient **scull**. He had been **discrete** about his **fined** as he was sure that his employer, who did not understand how important the artefact was, would attempt to **seas** it from him and **cell** it.

Cloze practice page 2 (page 100)

1. Sleep occurs in cycles. Each cycle has five **stages**. During the first and second stages, you sleep very lightly. Your breathing and heart **rate** become slower and **activity** in your body decreases, though you may still experience **occasional** muscle twitches. You begin to sleep more **deeply** during stages three and four. Your breathing becomes **rhythmic** and it is difficult for you to be woken by noise or other **disturbances**. The fifth stage of the cycle is when you dream. During this stage, your eyes **dart** about rapidly beneath your closed eyelids.

2. Three were men and one a woman, and all were oddly **dressed**. They wore round hats that rose to a small point a foot above their heads, with little **bells** around the **brims** that tinkled **sweetly** as they moved. The hats of the men were blue; the little woman's hat was white, and she wore a white **gown** that hung in pleats from her shoulders. Over it were **sprinkled** little stars that **glistened** in the sun like diamonds. The men were dressed in blue, of the same **shade** as their hats, and wore well-polished boots with a deep roll of blue at the tops.

Cloze practice page 3 (page 101)

1. Although the waiter had recommended **different** soup, I chose a **the** dish: *Although the waiter had recommended the soup, I chose a different dish.*

2. The storm began **ruined** and our picnic was **suddenly**: *The storm began suddenly and our picnic was ruined.*

3. We dusted the shelves **until** scrubbed the floor **and** it shone: *We dusted the shelves and scrubbed the floor until it shone.*

4. She could **whether** remember **not** she had locked the door: *She could not remember whether she had locked the door.*

5. **accessorise**
   Jason felt uncomfortable in his tight-fitting suit.

6. **dreaming**
   She leant back in the hammock and promptly fell asleep.

7. **to**
   It is a shame that you will not be able to attend this evening.

8. **icicles**
   Snow covered the fields in thick drifts which were ideal for sledging.

9. Matthew s <u>a</u> u n t <u>e</u> r e d leisurely past the f <u>o</u> u n t <u>a</u> i n. He was not due at the o <u>f</u> f i c e for another <u>h</u> o u <u>r</u> and he p l <u>a</u> n n e d to make the most of his time by e <u>x</u> p l <u>o</u> r i n g the <u>b</u> e <u>a</u> u t <u>i</u> f <u>u</u> l park.

10. **i)** summoned
    ii) entertain
    iii) found
    iv) complained
    v) bored

Number patterns

Number sequences (pages 102–105)

1. **23** (+ 3)

2. **10** (− 5 − 4 − 3 − 2 − 1)

3. **24** (+ 2 + 3 repeating)

4. **3** (− 3)

5. **16** (− 2 − 3 − 1 repeating)

6. **36** (+ 6 + 5 + 4 + 3 + 2)

7. **4** (− 6 − 5 − 4 repeating)

8. **9** (+ 4)

9. **33** (+ 3 + 4 + 5 + 6 + 7)

10. **36** (− 1 + 4 repeating)

11. **32** (× 2)

Schofield & Sims

Answers

12. **10** ($\div$ 2)

13. **81** ($\times$ 3)

14. **25** ($\div$ 2)

15. **600** ($\times$ 5 $\times$ 4 $\times$ 3 $\times$ 2)

16. **6** ($\div$ 2)

17. **1200** ($\times$ 5 $\times$ 4 $\times$ 3 $\times$ 2)

18. **5** ($\div$ 6 $\div$ 5 $\div$ 4 $\div$ 3)

19. **567** ($\times$ 3)   **20.** **0.12** ($\div$ 10)

21. **9** (leapfrogging, starting on 3, + 2 each time)

22. **15** (leapfrogging, starting on 30, − 5 each time)

23. **13** (adding the two previous numbers: 5 + 8)

24. **65** (adding the two previous numbers: 25 + 40)

25. **95** (doubling the amount adding each time:
+ 3 + 6 + 12 + 24 + 48, *or* doubling the number,
then adding 1: 2 $\times$ 2 = 4 + 1 = 5, 2 $\times$ 5 =
10 + 1 = 11, 2 $\times$ 11 = 22 + 1 = 23, etc.)

26. **15** (leapfrogging, starting on 120, $\div$ 2 each time)

27. **156** (adding the two previous numbers: 60 + 96)

28. **438** (doubling the amount added each time:
+ 14 + 28 + 56 + 112 + 224, *or* doubling the
number and then adding 10: 2 $\times$ 4 = 8 + 10 = 18,
2 $\times$ 18 = 36 + 10 = 46, 2 $\times$ 46 = 92 + 10 = 102,
etc.)

29. **9** (leapfrogging, starting on 1, + 2 each time)

30. **8** (leapfrogging, starting on 2, + 2 each time)

31. **343** (cube numbers: 3^3, 4^3, 5^3, 6^3, 7^3)

32. **100** (square numbers: 6^2, 7^2, 8^2, 9^2, 10^2)

33. **49** (square numbers: 3^2, 4^2, 5^2, 6^2, 7^2)

34. **8** (cube numbers: 6^3, 5^3, 4^3, 3^3, 2^3)

35. **16** (+ 4)   **36.** **3** ($\times$ 3)

37. **4** (+ 1, + 2, + 3, + 4, + 5)

38. **142** (− 20)

39. **16** (adding the two previous numbers: 6 + 10)

40. **15** (doubling the amount added each time
(+ 2 + 4 + 8 + 16 + 32, *or* doubling the number
and then adding 1: 2 $\times$ 1 = 2 + 1 = 3,
2 $\times$ 3 = 6 + 1 = 7, 2 $\times$ 7 = 14 + 1 = 15, etc.)

41. **30** (leapfrogging, starting on 40, − 10 each time)

42. **6** (adding the two previous numbers: 17 − 11 = 6,
or 5 + 6 = 11)

Letters for numbers (page 106)

1. **E** (16)   **5.** **30**   **9.** **52**

2. **E** (40)   **6.** **190**   **10.** **48**

3. **A** (3)   **7.** **576**   **11.** **CAB**

4. **C** (48)   **8.** **1**   **12.** **FED**

Missing number (pages 107–108)

1. **2**   **8.** **8**   **15.** **23**

2. **5**   **9.** **0**   **16.** **90**

3. **7**   **10.** **4**   **17.** **6**

4. **4**   **11.** **15**   **18.** **37**

5. **2**   **12.** **2**   **19.** **5**

6. **8**   **13.** **2**   **20.** **35**

7. **4**   **14.** **8**

Number connections (pages 109–111)

1. **24** (a $\times$ b)   **5.** **4** (b $\div$ a)

2. **20** (a + b)   **6.** **56** (a $\times$ b)

3. **19** (a − b)   **7.** **8** (a $\div$ b)

4. **15** (a $\times$ b)   **8.** **41** (a − b)

9. **48** (a $\times$ b, then $\times$ 2)

10. **27** (a + b, then + 1)

11. **14** (b − a, then − 1)

12. **12** (a + b, then $\div$ 2)

13. **14** (a $\div$ b, then + 10)

14. **15** (b − a, then − 1)

15. **17** (a $\div$ b, then + b)

16. **61** (a + b, then − 8)

17. **17** ($\div$ 2)

18. **103** (+ 10)

19. **18** ($\div$ 4)

20. **8** (find the square root)

21. **10.8** ($\div$ 10)

22. **97** (− 11)

23. **42** ($\times$ 3)

24. **7** ($\div$ 11, then − 1)

Number patterns practice page 1
(page 112)

1. **42** (+ 7)

2. **192** ($\times$ 2)

3. **36** (− 12)

4. **64** (all square numbers: the answer is 8^2)

5. **38** (+ 2 + 4 + 6 + 8 + 10)

6. **36** (leapfrogging, starting on 9, + 9 each time)

7. **159** (doubling the number added each time:
+ 5 + 10 + 20 + 40 + 80)

8. **156** (after the first two terms, add the previous
two terms)

Answers

Number patterns practice page 1

(page 112) continued

9. **30** (÷ 2)

10. **125** (all cube numbers: the answer is 5^3)

11. **1** (× 6, × 5, × 4, × 3, × 2)

12. **47** (× 2 then + 1 each time)

13. **2000** (÷ 10)

14. **84** (leapfrogging, starting on 108, − 12 each time)

15. **173** (halving the number subtracted each time: − 80, −40, − 20, − 10, − 5)

16. **E** (14)   22. **C** (−4)

17. **C** (28)   23. **A** (21)

18. **A** (3)   24. **E** (14)

19. **D** (2)   25. **204**

20. **B** (60)   26. **116**

21. **B** (66)   27. **6** (76 − 70)

Number patterns practice page 2

(page 113)

1. 5   6. 2   11. 7

2. 7   7. 39   12. 8

3. 36   8. 3   13. 6

4. 3   9. 97   14. 49

5. 2   10. 3   15. 1

16. **42** (a × b)   23. **30** (a + b, then − 10)

17. **33** (a + b)   24. **71** (a + b + b)

18. **47** (a − b)   25. **46** (a − b, then × 2)

19. **11** (a ÷ b)   26. **12** (a + b, then ÷ 3)

20. **38** (b − a)   27. **19** (b − a, then ÷ 2)

21. **80** (a ÷ b, then × 10)   28. **27** (× 3)

22. **27** (a × b, then − 1)   29. **53** (÷ 4)

Problem-solving

Number logic (page 114)

1. fourteen   6. one

2. nine   7. forty-five

3. ten   8. twenty-six

4. forty-eight   9. seventy-two

5. fifty   10. thirty-two

Days and dates (pages 115–116)

1. Friday   3. Wednesday   5. March

2. November   4. Sunday   6. February

7. Saturday

8. **Five** (2nd, 9th, 16th, 23rd and 30th March)

9. **Wednesday**

10. **Four** (3rd, 10th, 17th and 24th September)

11. **30th April**

12. **55 days** (30 days in November + 25 in December)

Time (page 118)

1. 8.40 a.m.

	Leaves	Time taken	Arrives
Pratik	8.20 a.m.		8.50 a.m.
Callum	8.30 a.m.		9.00 a.m.
Prianka	8.35 a.m.	20 min	8.55 a.m.
Chrissy	8.40 a.m.	15 min	8.55 a.m.

2. 45 minutes

	Starts	Time taken	Finishes
Salima	4.05 p.m.		5.45 p.m.
Rafi	4.35 p.m.	1hr 30 min	6.05 p.m.
Emmanuel	5 p.m.	45 min	5.45 p.m.

3. Brian

	Starts	Time taken	Finishes
Brian	1.25 p.m.	32 min	1.57 p.m.
Sheldon	1.33 p.m.	16 min	
Sidney		28 min	2.22 p.m.
Brenda	1.32 p.m.	25 min	1.57 p.m.

Position (page 120)

1. Shannon

V   B   H   J   S

2. Umar

back of the queue   *front of the queue*

Max   Jul   Lil   Ril   Bro   Teg   Uma

3. Kaiden and Darcie

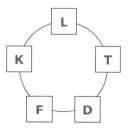

4. Lee   5. Taylor

Answers

Sorting information (pages 121–122)

1. **Three children** (Molly, Alex and Faiz)

	Ch	Ba	Fu	Va	St	Ra
Ma	/			/	/	
Mo		/	/	/		
Al	/	/	/			/
Su				/		
Fa	/	/	/			

2. **19 white paws**

   Remember that each kitten has four paws.

   2 kittens with brown stripes and white paws =
   2 × 4 = 8 white paws

   1 kitten with 1 black and 3 white paws =
   3 white paws

   1 kitten with grey stripes and white paws =
   4 white paws

   1 kitten with white all over = 4 white paws

   8 + 3 + 4 + 4 = 19

   (A sixth kitten has black paws and no white ones
   at all)

3. **Five children**

	Ha	Gl	Sc
A	/	/	
B		/	/
C	/		/
D	/	/	/
E			
F		/	/

4. **Three children** (Amy, Robert and Yan)

	Fl	Vi	Ce	Pi	Ha	Sa	Gu
Aj	/	/	/				
L				/	/	/	
Am	/	/		/		/	
R	/			/			/
Y	/		/	/	/		
B	/	/					

5. **1500g** or **1.5kg**

True statements (pages 123–124)

1. C
2. B
3. C
4. E
5. D
6. E

Problem-solving practice page 1

(page 125)

1. fourteen
2. seventy-seven
3. five
4. twenty-one
5. thirteen
6. fifty-seven
7. **December**

Juliette	Born five months earlier than May (when Martha was born) = December
Neema	Born in June
Martha	Born one month earlier than June (the month before Neema) = May

8. **September**

   Work out what month it would have been 18
   months earlier than March.

   March less 12 months = March. Take away another
   six months = September

9. **21st June**

   24th and 31st May will be Thursdays.

   Then the first three Thursdays in June will be the 7th,
   14th and 21st.

10. **11:55**

    Plane departs at 08:35 plus 20 minutes = 08:55.

    Flight arrives 08:55 plus 8 hours = 16:55 UK time.

    16:55 minus 5 hours = 11:55.

11. **40 minutes**

    The alarm clock goes off at 7.30 a.m. minus five
    minutes = 7.25 a.m.

    Rhys sleeps until 7.25 a.m. plus 15 minutes =
    7.40 a.m.

    He could get to school at 7.40 a.m. plus 25 minutes
    = 8.05 a.m.

    He doesn't have to be there until 8.45 a.m.

    So, he has 8.45 minus 8.05 = 40 minutes to get ready.

12. **18:25**

    The preparation will take 35 plus 25 plus 10 plus
    15 minutes = 1 hour and 25 minutes.

    I want the pizza ready at 19:45 plus 5 minutes =
    19:50.

    19:50 minus 1 hour and 25 minutes = 18:25.

Problem-solving practice page 2

(page 126)

1. **Sakshay**

   The order of the people in the queue is as follows:

   back of the queue   *front of the queue*

   Sashika   Bilal   Chloe   Maya   Joel   Sakshay

Problem-solving practice page 2

(page 126) continued

2. 750g (parcel C)

It is helpful at the start to convert the weights given in kilograms into grams.

Then all the weights are in the same units.

A	1.5kg = 1500g
B	1500g plus 0.25kg (250g) = 1750g
C	C = 1500g minus 750g = 750g
D	1500g plus 150g = 1650g
E	1650g plus 50g = 1700g

3. Mae

4. 20

	Che	Ghe	Chi	Let	Rel	Tom
Sa	/	/	/	/	X	/
Be	/	/	/			
Jo	/	/	/			
Ma	X	/	X	/	/	/
Rhi	/	/	/	/	X	/
Ang	X	X	X	X	X	X

5. One (car E)

	Saloon	Hatch	Estate	Stripe	Door col	Sunroof	Air con
A	/					/	
B		/				Either B or C has a sunroof	
C		/				/	
D	/					/	
E	/			/	/	/	/
F			/	/			/

6. 32 marbles (he gave 68 away)

Problem-solving practice page 3 (page 127)

1. C   **3. C**

2. D   **4. D**

Practice test (pages 129–141)

Alphabet positions

1. s   **2. n**   **3. e**

Alphabetical order

4. o   **5. attire**

Letter sequences

6. GI (+1 = G, +1 = I)

7. ZW (−2 = Z, −3 = W)

Letter codes

8. QV (numbered 10, 5)   **9. CA** (+4, −6)

Word codes

10. VOJOGT (+3, +2, +1, +3, +2, +1)

11. LATHE

12. SLHGROV (letter partners)

Match the codes

13. 3768   4719   4583
     HUGS   RUNT   RASH
   i) 6583   **ii) 89716**

Make a word from one other word

14. (demean mend) (easier sire) (harass **rash**)

15. (breeze beer) (recite rice) (strong **sort**)

Make a word from two other words

16. (built [**dial**] aside) (deeds [**need**] event)

17. (office [**fairy**] starry) (access [**cream**] scream)

Word meanings

18. C (religious)   **19. E** (urge)

Sort words into groups

20. i)   D (type of building material)
   ii)   A (type of bird)
   iii) B (type of flower)
   iv) C (type of weather)
   v)   B (type of flower)
   vi) C (type of weather)

Ordering words

21. county (physical size: **village, town, county, country, continent**)

22. chicken (physical size: **sparrow, raven, chicken, swan, ostrich**)

23. cylinder (number of faces: **sphere, cone, cylinder, tetrahedron, cuboid**)

Synonyms

24. (ordinary **aristocracy** ability) (**nobility** remarkable temporary)

25. ultimately   **26. restrain**

Antonyms

27. affix, detach   **28. appear**   **29. plural**

Answers

Synonym and antonym grid

30. i) invigorated, alert, energetic
   ii) squirm, wriggle
   iii) mean, inconsiderate
   iv) tall, giant, towering

Analogies

31. Clam is to (broth, overfill, **shellfish**) as weasel is to (stoat, **mammal**, cunning).

32. Guest is to (host, **guessed**, hotel) as mews is to (kitten, entertain, **muse**).

33. Reply is to (respond, **rely**, telegram) as skate is to (board, stroll, **sate**).

Odd ones out

34. bough, precipice (the others are all rock sizes)

35. traditional, revival (the others are all synonyms)

36. infection, illness (the others are all types of fuel)

Word connections

37. squash

38. hatch

Singular and plural

39. buses

40. feet

41. possibilities

42. successes

Root words, prefixes and suffixes

43. act

44. phobia

45. immature

46. afterwards

Word classes

47. The shoes belong **to** Christine.

48.

Collective noun	Adjective	Adverb	Verb
set	old	rarely	looked

49. despite

Word tenses

50. Dogs howled outside.

51. travelling

Missing letter

52. r (tender, ratio, error, relish)

53. b (daub, broad, bulb, bowl)

Move a letter

54. d (boar, noted)

55. l (quit, place)

Word ladders

56. HINT, HUNT

57. GLOW, BLOW *or* BROW, BLOW

Missing three letters

58. OWL (howled)

59. RAN (grandma)

60. PEN (spent)

61. ICE (rice)

Words with letters in common

62. ascend

63. sore, rose

Spot the word

64. Some child**ren t**hink teachers know everything. (**rent**) ('weve' is not a correct answer because the contraction 'we've' requires an apostrophe.)

65. The views **alt**er depending on the light. (**salt**)

66. My team cho**se al**l the best players (**seal**)

67. Felt tips for sale – fi**ve in** a packet! (**vein**)

Join two words to make one

68. (with **rat** moth) (**her** our herd) (rather)

69. ant (important, pleasant, triumphant)

Add or remove a letter to make a new word

70. s (silk, said, surge, sharp)

71. curse (remove o)

Spot spelling mistakes

72. spectre   **73.** confirm   **74.** appreciate

Anagrams

75. LEAFLET, COLOURFUL   **76.** LEARNED

Find the letter missing from the muddled words

77. o (The scientist did not DOUBT that her THEORY was correct.)

78. y (Once the flowers begin to DECAY, you must EMPTY the vase.)

Word grids

79.

L	A	P	S	E	D
L	■		C	■	O
A	N	T	H	E	M
M	■		I	■	A
A	■		S	■	I
S	T	A	M	E	N

Answers

Select words to complete a sentence

80. The tourists decided that there was (plenty, **little**, always) to see in the city, so they went (**hiking**, climb, trudged) in the countryside (although, moreover, **instead**).

81. **C** (My supportive colleagues **signed** my petition eagerly.)

Homophones

82. **brows, sum, board**

83. The **bawled** man was painting the **sealing** with white paint.

Select words to complete a paragraph

84. I was quite happy in my new place, and if there was one thing that I missed it must not be thought I was **i) discontented**; all who had to do with me were good and I had a light airy **ii) stable** and the best of food. What more could I want? Why, liberty! For three years and a half of my life I had had all the **iii) liberty** I could wish for; but now, week after **iv) week**, month after month, and no doubt year after year, I must stand up in a stable night and **v) day** except when I am **vi) wanted**, and then I must be just as **vii) steady** and quiet as any old horse who has worked twenty **viii) years**.

Rearrange words to make a sentence

85. She sipped the hot **carefully coffee**.
She sipped the hot coffee carefully.

86. The **from** stooped to drink **giraffe** the pool.
The giraffe stooped to drink from the pool.

Find the superfluous word

87. **no**
Sophie found it difficult to accept that she must apologise for her behaviour.

88. **walking**
I trembled as I listened to the slow footsteps approaching the door.

Complete the word

89. The **i)** s c **i** e n t **i** s t carefully added the **ii)** p o **w** d e r to the flask and watched as the **iii)** m **i** x t **u r** e began to **iv)** f **o a** m. She had not conducted this **v)** e x p e r **i m** e n t before and she was **vi)** e **x** c i t **e** d to see the **vii)** r e **s u** l t s.

90. **i)** ornament   **iv)** attention
    ii) thud   **v)** feigned
    iii) attempting

Number sequences

91. **0.25** (× 10)

92. **24** (leapfrogging, starting on 18, + 6 each time)

93. **102** (after the first two terms, add the previous two terms)

Letters for numbers

94. **E** (34)   **95. D** (75)   **96. 73**

Missing number

97. 85   **98. 8**

Number connections

99. 65 (a + 2b)   **100. 19** (a ÷ 10 + b)

Number logic

101. Ninety-nine   **102. Twenty**

Days and dates

103. Tuesday

104. Four (on 3rd, 10th, 17th and 24th November)

Time

105. Fifteen minutes

106. 22:35
Plane departs at 18:05 plus 7 hours and 40 minutes = 01:45.
Flight arrives 01:45 plus 1 hour and 50 minutes = 03:35 UK time.
03:35 minus five hours = 22:35.

Position

107. James
The order of the boys' heights is as follows:
shortest   *tallest*
James   Zaid   David   Ayan   Leo   Neil

Sorting information

108. Thursday

109. 7 people who paid by card
At the start there are 16 people on the bus = 9 paid by cash and 7 paid by card.
At the first stop, 7 people get off the bus = 3 paid by cash and 4 paid by card.
There are therefore 9 people on the bus = 6 paid by cash and 3 paid by card.
Then 8 people get on the bus = 4 paid by cash and 4 paid by card.
There are therefore 17 people on the bus = 10 paid by cash and 7 paid by card.

True statements

110. E   **111. A**

Index and Glossary

adjacent 72, 105 — next to, neighbouring, on either side of

alternate 13 — to happen in turns – first one, then the other – or next but one

analogy (pl. **analogies**) 46–48, 55, 132 — a way of comparing similar things

antonym (pl. **antonyms**) 41–45, 54, 132 — a word that means the opposite of another (so **new** is an antonym of **old**)

BODMAS 108 — where there are several calculations to do in an **equation**, the **mnemonic** reminds you of the **sequence**: the sum inside the **B**rackets, **O**rder (anything to the **power** of something), **D**ivision, **M**ultiplication, **A**ddition, **S**ubtraction

calculate, calculation 103, 106–109 — to work something out using numbers

connection 14, 34, 36, 38, 46–48, 50, 55, 58, 97, 109–111, 113, 133, 140 — a link between two or more things

connective 59, 62, 96, 134 — a word or phrase that connects two clauses in a sentence (for example, **and**, **but** or **or**)

consecutive 14, 68, 105 — next to others (for example, in a **sequence** or list) with no gaps

cubed 104 — describes a number that is multiplied by itself twice and is shown by the number ^{3} (for example, 3^3, or 3 to the **power** of 3, is $3 \times 3 \times 3 = 27$ and 27 is a cubed number)

deduce 123 — to work something out using other facts that you already know

equation 107, 108, 113, 139 — a number statement showing that two amounts or values are the same

homonym 145, 146, 147 — a word that sounds the same as another word and is spelt the same, but has a different meaning

homophone 48, 89, 92, 99, 137 — a word that sounds the same as another word, but is spelt differently

horizontal 69 — going across from left to right or right to left so that it is level, like the floor or the horizon

identify 5–8, 22, 27, 32–34, 36, 53, 56–59, 67, 70, 71, 77, 81, 89, 92, 93, 97, 109, 110, 114, 115, 123, 125, 131 — to find something, to notice the ways in which it is different or to find out exactly what it is

in common 22, 34, 49, 70, 71, 86, 135 — having some of the same features

inverse 107 — the reverse or opposite

leapfrog, leapfrogging 13, 103 — to jump over, as in a game of leapfrogging

Index and Glossary

location 27, 28

place, position

logic 4, 114, 125, 140

a way of thinking in which you use facts that you know to find other facts that are less obvious

mnemonic 108

a saying that helps you to remember something that might otherwise be difficult to remember

odd ones out 49, 55, 133

those that are different from all the others

operation 103, 107, 109–111

a specific activity or method of working (for example, multiplication and division are operations)

order(ing) 9–11, 25, 29, 36, 48, 53, 65, 68, 69, 81, 86, 88, 96, 108, 129, 131, 135, 136

1. The way in which a set of items is arranged
2. a mathematical **operation** that involves multiplying a number by itself (for example, 6^2, 2^3)

power 108

to the power of is to do with the number of times a number is to be multiplied by itself (for example, 4 to the power of 2 is 4^2 or 4×4)

prefix (pl. **prefixes**) 32, 33, 57, 61, 75, 133

one or more letters added to the start of the word to change its meaning (so **un** + **kind** = **unkind**)

scan 37, 41, 45–48

to look at something quickly, without thinking too hard about it

sequence (pl. **sequences**) 4, 12–14, 30, 36, 53, 102–105, 112, 129, 131, 139

the special **order** in which a particular set or **series** of items is arranged

series 12–14, 30, 102, 129

a set of items arranged in a special **order** or **sequence**

sort(ing) 34, 35, 52, 58, 121, 122, 126, 131, 141

to arrange, organise or separate

squared 104

describes a number that is multiplied by itself once and is shown by the number ^{2} (for example, 5^2, or 5 to the **power** of 2, is $5 \times 5 = 25$, and 25 is a squared number)

suffix (pl. **suffixes**) 33, 57, 61, 75, 133

one or more letters added to the end of a word to change its meaning (so **use** + **less** = **useless**)

synonym (pl. **synonyms**) 37–41, 45, 53, 54, 131, 132

a word meaning the same or almost the same as another (so **moist** is a synonym of **damp**)

trial and error 119

a way of solving a problem by trying out several possible answers to see if any of them work

vocabulary 4, 32, 34, 35, 51–55, 66, 79, 81, 97

a collection of words – sometimes those related to a particular subject

Schofield & Sims